COLLECTION MANAGEMENT

8/27/13	0 ~ 1	

Mary Eliza Mahoney
and the Legacy of
African-American Nurses

Women in Medicine

Karen Horney
Pioneer of Feminine Psychology

Mathilde Krim and the Story of AIDS

Elisabeth Kübler-Ross
Encountering Death and Dying

Rita Levi-Montalcini
Nobel Prize Winner

Mary Eliza Mahoney
and the Legacy of African-American Nurses

Margaret Sanger
Rebel for Women's Rights

WOMEN in MEDICINE

Mary Eliza Mahoney and the Legacy of African-American Nurses

Susan Muaddi Darraj

CHELSEA HOUSE
PUBLISHERS
A Haights Cross Communications Company
Philadelphia

COVER: Mary Eliza Mahoney (1845–1926). Mahoney was the first black woman to graduate from nursing school in the United States. She received her diploma in August 1879 from the New England Hospital for Women and Children in Boston and became a major advocate for abolishing injustice to blacks in the nursing profession.

CHELSEA HOUSE PUBLISHERS
VP, NEW PRODUCT DEVELOPMENT Sally Cheney
DIRECTOR OF PRODUCTION Kim Shinners
CREATIVE MANAGER Takeshi Takahashi
MANUFACTURING MANAGER Diann Grasse

Staff for MARY ELIZA MAHONEY AND THE LEGACY OF AFRICAN-AMERICAN NURSES
EXECUTIVE EDITOR Lee M. Marcott
PHOTO EDITOR Sarah Bloom
PRODUCTION EDITOR Noelle Nardone
SERIES & COVER DESIGNER Takeshi Takahashi
LAYOUT 21st Century Publishing and Communications, Inc.

A Haights Cross Communications ⟋ Company

http://www.chelseahouse.com

First Printing

9 8 7 6 5 4 3 2 1

Library of Congress Cataloging-in-Publication Data

Darraj, Susan Muaddi.
  Mary Eliza Mahoney and the legacy of African-American nurses/
by Susan Muaddi Darraj.
    p. cm.—(Women in medicine)
  ISBN 0-7910-8029-3
  1. Mahoney, Mary Eliza, 1845–1926. 2. African-American nurses—
History. 3. African-American nurses—Biography. 4. Nursing—United
States—History. I. Title. II. Series.
RT83.5.D37 2004
610.73'089'96073—dc22

J 610.73
m216
(B)

2004008474

All links and web addresses were checked and verified to be correct at the time of publication. Because of the dynamic nature of the web, some addresses and links may have changed since publication and may no longer be valid.

Table of Contents

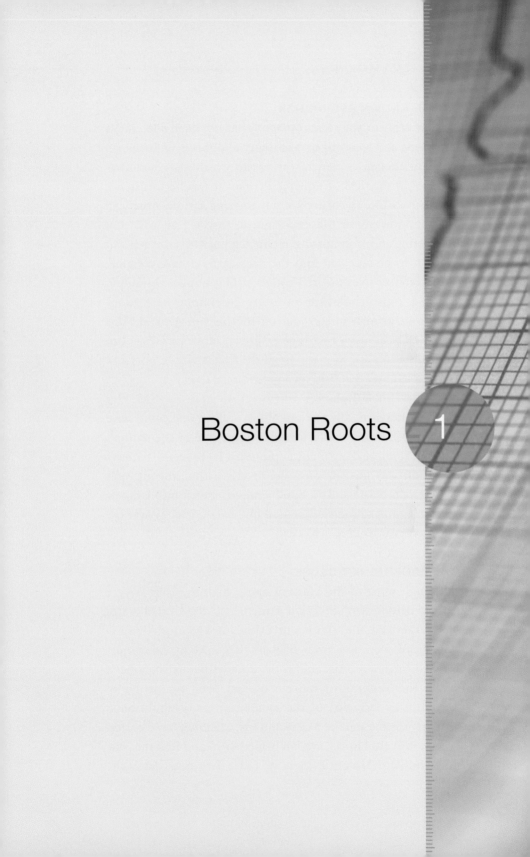

Boston Roots 1

LITTLE-KNOWN BEGINNINGS

The life story of Mary Eliza Mahoney has not been adequately preserved and recorded by historians, and this is unfortunate. Perhaps racism caused historians to overlook her contributions to the field of nursing. Perhaps it was her insistence on a private life. The history of this amazing African-American woman, however, is too important to forget. Her work and pioneering efforts in nursing and in helping African-American women to be accepted into the nursing field have certainly impacted our lives today. Though little is known about her, she had a great influence on future generations of African-American women nurses and on the field in general. This book will be as much a study of the history of African-American women in nursing as it will be of the first African-American woman to enter that field on a professional level.

Mary Eliza Mahoney was born on May 7, 1845. Her birth garnered hardly any attention, and no one could have predicted that the infant would become one of the nation's most groundbreaking medical pioneers. In 1845, the nation's attention was focused on a major crisis: the growing split between the North and the South. Indeed, at the time Mahoney was born, the nation was focused on heated debates over the controversial issue of slavery.

THE ABOLITIONIST CAUSE

Although most of the Western world had given up slavery (Great Britain had abolished it in 1833),[1] the United States still practiced the abhorrent crime of keeping African-American men and women in bondage. Many Americans worked to change this, and in the decades before Mahoney's birth, the abolitionist movement had been increasing in strength. In fact, one of the major centers of abolitionist activity was the state of Massachusetts, Mahoney's birthplace. There, William Lloyd Garrison helped form and lead the New England Anti-Slavery Society in 1831. Two years later, the

American Anti-slavery Society was established, also a result of Garrison's efforts. Both societies were largely composed of male membership (in later years, women would join and even become leaders of the movement) and called for an end to slavery without compensation to slave owners. Garrison and his organizations objected to the institution of slavery on two points. Slavery violated Christian teachings, and it made a mockery of democracy.[2] Garrison began publishing a newspaper called *The Liberator*.[3] Headquartered in Boston, the newspaper became the main publication of the abolitionist movement; it featured editorials and articles that sought to change America's attitude towards slavery.

FREDERICK DOUGLASS

One of the legends of the African-American community, Frederick Douglass, also made Massachusetts his headquarters, finding sympathetic friends and colleagues in its citizenry. It has been suggested that Douglass and Mary Eliza Mahoney were actually distant relatives. Douglass was born a slave in Maryland and was separated from his mother as an infant. His mother was also a slave, but Douglass suspected that his father was a white man. This fact, however, did not protect him from the harsh life of a slave. He grew up watching other slaves, including some who were related to him, endure harsh and unfair punishments at the hands of their white foremen or plantation owners. These punishments included severe beatings that left the slaves physically maimed and emotionally scarred. The abuse, however, went even further.

As a young boy, Douglass was sent by his owner to serve in the home of the Auld family of Baltimore. Mrs. Auld treated him kindly, often including him in the school lessons she gave to her own young son, Thomas. She taught Douglass the alphabet and how to put the letters together to form simple words. The lessons were discovered and interrupted by Mr. Auld. The master of the house, furious that his wife had been trying to educate one of their slaves, fumed: "If you give a nigger an inch, he will take an ell. A nigger should know nothing but to obey his master—to do as he is told to do. Learning would *spoil* the best nigger in the world. . . . It would forever unfit him to be a slave."[4] Douglass would never forget those words.

Later in his life, Douglass escaped from the South to the North, settling in the Boston area. He became a regular speaker on the abolitionist circuit, railing against the evils of slavery and emphasizing the ways in which the racist institution corrupted the morals of African Americans as well as those of white Americans. He also wrote his autobiography in 1845, *The Narrative of the Life of Frederick Douglass, an American Slave*, which became a best-selling book.

So impressive was he, so articulate were his descriptions of the lives of slaves in the South, that many audiences questioned his authenticity. How, they wondered, could an illiterate slave speak and write so well? The secret to overcoming oppression, as Douglass learned from Mr. Auld on that day in Baltimore, was in education. Mr. Auld's anger at the thought of an educated slave made Douglass think: "I now understand what had been to me a most perplexing difficulty—to wit, the white man's power to enslave the black man. It was a grand achievement, and I prized it highly. From that moment, I understood the pathway from slavery to freedom."[5]

Indeed, since the day Mr. Auld had obstructed his learning, Douglass had pursued an education, often having to rely on his own sense of discipline and ingenuity to do so. He taught himself how to read, building upon the foundation he had gleaned from Mrs. Auld. By the time Douglass died, he was respected in Boston and across the nation as a paragon of possibility—an example of what African Americans could do if given an opportunity. Many young African Americans, including Mary Eliza Mahoney, undoubtedly viewed the life of Frederick Douglass as an example of the kind of social mobility that was possible if one sought an education.

HARRIET BEECHER STOWE

By the 1950s, New England had become a hub of abolitionist activity and discussion. It was in this environment that one of the most important books of the era was written, one that would contribute to the momentum of antislavery sentiment.[6]

Born in Connecticut in 1811, Harriet Beecher Stowe was raised in a religious family. Her father and brother were Protestant clergymen, and Harriet herself eventually married a clergyman. Her mother died when Harriet was a child, but her religious father raised her and took charge of her education. While he schooled her in Puritan theology and Biblical studies, he also encouraged her to read classical writers, such as William Shakespeare. Stowe married and moved to Maine where she gave birth to and raised seven children. As a religious woman, she saw slavery as an inherently evil social institution that morally corrupted any who were involved in it.[7] She decided to write a novel that depicted her abolitionist views.

The result of her literary efforts was *Uncle Tom's Cabin*, which was published in 1851 in *National Era*, a journal dedicated to antislavery ideals. The novel, published in book form in 1852, tells the story of a middle-aged slave who was sold by his master and separated from his wife and family. It depicts the vile system of slavery that caused many African Americans to suffer but also makes a point of portraying Uncle Tom as a true example of a devout Christian.[8]

Uncle Tom's Cabin sparked a mixed reaction—acclaim from Northern readers and dismay from Southern readers. Southerners loudly protested the novel's portrayal of the white, aristocratic, slave-owning class of the South as morally corrupt and un-Christian.[9] They also questioned the details and accuracy of the book. Nonetheless, *Uncle Tom's Cabin*—and its author—rose to prominence in both the United States and Europe where the novel was also a bestseller. It was eventually translated into more than 20 languages and reached a wide and varied audience. Stowe's literary success led to financial wealth, and the family bought a home in Andover, Massachusetts, where they lived between 1852 and 1864. Stowe continued writing and produced another abolitionist novel, *Dred: A Tale of the Dismal Swamp,* as well as work in other genres. The presence of Harriet Beecher Stowe in New England was an integral part of the abolitionist atmosphere in which Mary Eliza Mahoney grew up.[10]

RACISM IN BOSTON

Some accounts say Mary Eliza Mahoney was born in Dorchester while others claim that she was born in Roxbury, Massachusetts, but the fact remains that she spent most of her formative years in Boston. Although Boston was known as a major hub of abolitionist sentiment and action, it was not an ideal environment for African Americans. As one contemporary writer explained, "Boston's abolitionists spoke from the *Liberator's* pages. But what was espoused and what was possible often were quite different."[11]

In the late 1600s, Boston had been a major center of the slave trade. By the early 1700s, African Americans were permitted to buy their own freedom, and a class of free, working-class African Americans soon emerged in Boston. Crispus Attucks, an African American, was the first person to die in the Boston Massacre of 1770, the first casualty of the American Revolution. Massachusetts finally abolished slavery in 1783. Despite the slow but steady changes, many challenges for African Americans remained.[12]

Indeed, racism and discrimination were still widely practiced in Boston. Furthermore, African Americans in Boston were a minority—at the time of Mahoney's birth, only 2,000 of the city's 114,366 citizens were African Americans.[13] Even while much work and fanfare focused on the liberation of slaves, Boston's African-American citizens had little freedom and opportunity in their everyday lives. At the time of Mahoney's birth, African-American children could not attend schools with white children. The law supporting this racist tradition was repealed in 1855 when it was determined by the Boston Primary School Committee that "Distinction on account of race, color or religion in admission to public schools is forbidden."[14] Mahoney was then 10 years old.

Tension existed between African Americans and whites, especially between African-American and Irish-American Bostonians. In *Mary Eliza Mahoney, 1845–1926: America's First Black Professional Nurse,* author Helen Miller wrote that in the decade before Mahoney was born, approximately 50,000 legal and illegal Irish immigrants had flowed into the Massachusetts port city.[15] The numbers increased in succeeding years, and the recently landed Irish had trouble finding work and often lived in squalor. Miller pointed out that tension between the two communities arose partly because the African-American citizens had been well organized for many years and had established themselves. Even though they were outnumbered by the Irish, "the black minority, at that time, had the advantage of organization, leadership ability and occupational skills."[16] Although the Irish had trouble finding jobs, the unemployment rate among African Americans was quite low, leading to accusations that African Americans were "stealing" jobs from the Irish.

Another major point of tension was the Civil War, which loomed on the horizon in the mid-1840s and was to erupt in 1861. Abolitionists in Boston were gaining a visible platform against slavery, and African-American Bostonians thrived politically in this atmosphere. The new Irish immigrants, however, did not want the South to secede from the North, and they generally supported the institution of slavery.[17] Hostility mounted with the onset of the potato famine in Ireland. The famine began in the year of Mahoney's birth, 1845, and caused millions to flee the European island in search of opportunity. Most came to the United States, settling in the northeastern part of the country.

The conflict between Boston's African-American and Irish-American communities would characterize the atmosphere in which Mahoney grew up—where African Americans were accepted by some, but hardly all, of the population. This tepid acceptance made African Americans determined to prove themselves and overcome the obstacles of racism.

THE MAHONEY FAMILY

Although Mahoney's work as a professional nurse had a significant impact on that field, little is known about her personal life. Most sources note that she was the first African-American professional nurse but rarely go into more depth. The details of her life, and of her family's history, are scantily recorded.

Mahoney was born in 1845 to Peter Mahoney and Mary Jane Stewart Mahoney, both originally from North Carolina. It is presumed that they fled that state in order to escape the harshness of the slave system. Massachusetts had voted to abolish slavery in 1783 and had given African Americans the right to vote in 1840, so the Mahoneys, like many others, sought to make a new home there. (Some sources suggest that the Mahoneys may have lived in Nova Scotia for a short time, but there is no solid evidence to confirm this).[18]

The family had little money, and everyone was expected to work. Mahoney had one brother, Charles, and two sisters, Ellen and Louise, the latter of whom died as an adolescent. Precious little else is known about the family although Mahoney's descendants claimed to be related to the great abolitionist, Frederick Douglass.[19]

MORAL INSTRUCTION

A Baptist, Mahoney was a religious young woman. An enthusiastic churchgoer, she participated in many events of the People's Baptist Church in Roxbury, including a popular event called a "fishpond."[20] As a child, she attended the Phillips Street School, named after Boston's first mayor, John Phillips.[21] When she was four years old, Massachusetts passed legislation that offered a public school education to all African-American and white children in the state. [22] The desegregation law that was passed in 1855, when Mahoney was 10 years old, allowed for African-American and white children to attend the same schools. The Phillips Street School is famous for being the first desegregated school in the region. Mahoney attended the school from first through fourth grades. The year's tuition cost $15, and the school offered a challenging and rigorous program[23] that included English, Arithmetic, Physiology, Speech and Writing, and History, among other subjects. According to Miller, students at the Phillips Street School were also instructed in matters of morality:

> Moral instruction given included the infinite value of a love of truth, of justice, of integrity[,] of fidelity in contracts, of personal purity. It was also thought that charitableness in judgement must be earnestly inculcated. Such was the foundation Mary Mahoney received and upon which her career in nursing was built.[24]

Given the schooling she received in morals and humanitarian values, it is not surprising that Mahoney later pursued a degree in nursing, which was considered a noble calling. Perhaps Mahoney was attracted to nursing as a profession on the basis of its altruistic character and quality. The importance of nursing probably became evident to her in 1861, the year that the Civil War erupted. She was almost 16 years old at the time.

NORTH VS. SOUTH

The Civil War officially began on April 12, 1861—four days before Mahoney's sixteenth birthday—when Confederate soldiers attacked Fort Sumter in South Carolina. The cause of the attack helps to explain the cause of the war itself. (For more on this famous fort, enter "Fort Sumter" into any search engine and browse the sites listed.)

Abraham Lincoln became America's president in 1860, to the dismay and anger of Southerners, who saw his administration as a threat to their economy. Lincoln was known to consider slavery an evil institution. He publicly called it "a moral, a social, and a political wrong," but the entire southern economy heavily depended upon slavery.[25] Determined to break away from the Union and to form their own nation, the Confederate states began to secede. South Carolina seceded first; when it did so, the Union army stationed in South Carolina feared attack and moved its troops to Fort Sumter, believing it to be less vulnerable to attack because it lay further away from the Atlantic shore in the Charleston Harbor. In spite of their hopes, the Union troops were attacked by Confederate troops in an assault that lasted a day and a half.

Though no soldiers on either side were killed, the attack on Fort Sumter, which surrendered to the Confederacy on April 14, signaled an irreversible course of action. The South had officially attacked the North, and this launched the two sides into a war that threatened to ruin the dream of a United States; the nation was not yet 100 years old.

OPPOSING LIFESTYLES

The two regions of the nation differed in numerous ways, chiefly in their economy. As an agricultural economy, the South used slaves to keep its cotton export business bustling, producing massive quantities without paying for labor. The North, however, had become an industrial economy; manufactured goods formed the basis of its economic prosperity. Its factories were filled with paid employees not slaves. These differences sparked intense hostility between North and South, because Northerners' rejection of slavery was perceived as a threat to the "Southern way of life" and to the South's financial base.

CASUALTY RATES

The Civil War was memorable for many reasons, of course, but one of the lesser-known ones is the technological advances of the time. Some of the latest technology included the telegraph and modern weaponry. The rifle musket, for example, forever changed the way wars were fought. Previous models of the musket, and other firing weapons, had a range of no more than 300 feet. The rifle musket, however, could reach 900 feet—making the rate of casualties higher and the war more deadly.[26] For example, in the Battle of Perryville, Kentucky, on October 8, 1862, Union and Confederate losses amounted to 7,600 in one day.[27] In the battle of Shiloh, Tennessee, casualties on both sides totaled 23,700 lives—shocking the nation. During the Battle of Antietam on September 17, 1862, over 23,000 men were killed. By the end of the Civil War, over 600,000 lives would be lost.

Those soldiers who survived these and other vicious battles often wished they had been killed like their comrades. The rate of disease—and its rapid spread through military bases and camps—appalled many. Soldiers who had enlisted in the military with glorious ideas of fighting for the liberty of their region were quickly stripped of these illusions when they encountered the reality of war. That reality included vermin-infested camps, a scarcity of medicines for injuries and infections, unsanitary living conditions, and exhausting days filled with skirmishes, training, and backbreaking work. The bright spot in the lives of these disillusioned soldiers was often the presence of nurses.

2 Angels of Mercy

NURSING'S ORIGINS

In many ways, Mary Eliza Mahoney's home state of Massachusetts was a fortuitous place in which to grow up, for it was here that the field of nursing in America firmly entrenched itself and developed. It was a field Mahoney would help change forever.

At the time, nursing was a newly emerging profession. The late 1850s and early 1860s were also a time when the possibility of a young African-American woman entering the nursing profession coincided with the outbreak of the American Civil War, during which the need for professionally trained nurses became obvious.

Historically, nursing has been a female occupation, one of several reasons it is unique. To understand Mary Eliza Mahoney's entry into nursing, it is important to understand how nursing itself first emerged as a career track for women. For this, one must turn to Victorian England. When Queen Victoria ascended to the throne in 1837, she shaped the way women were expected to behave. The queen, through her own habits, encouraged women to focus on domesticity—to make the home and family the center of their lives. The Victorian culture that developed during her decades-long reign frowned upon women who sought an alternative life path that diverged from marriage and motherhood.

THE LADY WITH THE LAMP

Florence Nightingale was one young woman who went against these entrenched social norms and expectations. Rather than waste her time indulging in gossip, worrying about her appearance and clothes, and attending balls and galas like other young women of her generation and social class, Nightingale wanted something much more fulfilling. According to Darlene R. Stille, "This young English lady was deeply troubled by the sickness and poverty she saw around her. At the age of sixteen, she felt called by God to do something about it." [28]

13

Nightingale led a privileged life. Born in 1820 to very wealthy parents who owned a lot of land and who enjoyed foreign travel, she received a top-quality education. Rather than wasting this education on idle conversation with her social circle, she sought to put it to good use. All too soon, her thirst for making a difference in the world collided with the expectations of her parents—and of society. She took an interest in the people who lived and worked on her parents' estate and who were sick or ailing. She took satisfaction from tending to their needs. It was a "hobby" that quickly alarmed her parents.

When she expressed an interest in visiting sick people in the local hospitals, her parents outright forbade her to do so. At that time, hospitals were hardly cheerful places—poor sanitary conditions and cramped quarters meant that only the very poor sought medical care there. Wealthy people could afford to have doctors pay house calls. It was not just their daughter's desire to visit hospitals that upset the Nightingales. They were also disturbed by her general frame of mind and her reluctance to participate in popular pastimes that other young women of her class enjoyed. M. Patricia Donahue, author of *Nursing, The Finest Art: An Illustrated History*, observed, "Not surprisingly, [the Nightingales] hoped that she would give up her unusual ambition, marry, and continue in the social circles to which she was accustomed, and have children."[29] Little did they know that their daughter would eventually cause a medical revolution.

In 1844, Nightingale went against her parents' wishes and began visiting hospital-bound patients.[30] Everyone's warnings about the condition of the hospitals were correct:

> English hospitals were filthy and crowded. The nurses were uneducated, untrained, and poorly paid. Often, they were drunk on the job and treated patients cruelly. Diseases spread rapidly in the dirty hospital wards, because no one knew that germs cause disease and

infection. Any sick person who went to a hospital could expect to die rather than to get well.[31]

Full of ideas for plans to improve the conditions of these hospitals, Nightingale enrolled in a three-month nursing program in Germany in 1847. Six years later, in 1853, she traveled to Paris, France, to undergo training by the Sisters of Charity, an order of Roman Catholic nuns recognized for their care of the ill and poor.[32] She carefully observed their methods and noted the strict attention they paid to the cleanliness of their hospital facilities. For Nightingale, it became very clear that a clean environment led to a decrease in disease and infection and death rates. She planned to dedicate her life to improving hospital conditions and care for patients.

WOMEN'S CHOICES

Florence Nightingale's dedication came at a heavy personal cost. The Victorian era was not one in which women could maintain a marriage and family as well as a career. Nightingale had caught the eye of an English gentleman who proposed marriage to the young woman. According to Stille, "She was very fond of him and would have accepted his marriage proposal, but she feared that marriage would interfere with her calling to serve the poor and sickly. Finally, she had to reject him, which sent her into a deep depression."[33] Such a situation was not uncommon for many of the earliest advocates of the nursing field, including Mary Eliza Mahoney. These women would find themselves having to choose between their career ambitions and their desire to be married and have a family. Such a choice put many nurses to the test.

THE CRIMEAN WAR

Nightingale was serving as superintendent of an English hospital and establishing norms and high standards for nurses when the Crimean War began. In 1854, Great Britain, allied with France and Turkey, waged war against Russia in the region known as the Crimea. The war proved to be an arduous one for the British, and the dangers endured by soldiers became known because newspaper journalists reported the events and wrote detailed stories about how wounded soldiers died of poor care and disease. According to one news report, the conditions were abominable. The writer believed this would greatly upset the confidence of the British people in their army:

> It is with feelings of surprise and anger that the public will learn that no sufficient preparations have been made for the proper care of the wounded. Not only are there not sufficient surgeons ... not only are there no dressers and nurses ... there is not even linen to make bandages ... it is found that the commonest appliances of a workhouse sick-ward are wanting, and that the men must die through the medical staff of the British army having forgotten that old rags are necessary for the dressing of wounds.... The manner in which the sick and wounded are treated is worthy only of the savages of Dahomey.... Here the French are greatly our superiors. Their medical arrangements are extremely good, their surgeons are more numerous, and they have also the help of the Sisters of Charity, who have accompanied the expedition in incredible numbers. These devoted women are excellent nurses.[34]

Plagued by negative press and a furious public, the British Secretary of War, Sir Sidney Herbert, considered what to do. He was a friend of the Nightingales, and he knew about Florence and her meticulous work in British hospitals. He immediately wrote to her:

> There is but one person in England that I know of who would be capable of organising and superintending such a scheme.... You would of course have plenary

[absolute] authority over all the nurses, and I think I could secure you the fullest assistance and cooperation from the medical staff, and you would also have an unlimited power of drawing on the Government for whatever you thought requisite for the success of your mission...but I must not conceal from you that I think upon your decision will depend the ultimate success or failure of the plan. Your own personal qualities, your knowledge and your power of administration, and among greater things your rank and position in Society give you advantages in such a work which no other person possesses.[35]

As the new Superintendent of the Female Nursing Establishment of the English General Hospitals in Turkey, Nightingale sailed for Turkey with 38 nurses. The army hospital she found was like something in a nightmare: 3,000-4,000 men were crammed into a space meant to accommodate no more than 1,700. The facility lacked water, soap, clean clothing, and towels. Even worse, "an open sewer that attracted rats and vermin was immediately under the building."[36] The death rate was close to 50 percent, a dismal statistic.

Despite the fact that those in military command of the base in Turkey resented her presence—as a civilian and as a woman—Nightingale took charge of the grim situation she found. She ordered and organized the hospital, putting into place a system for checking regularly on patients and ensuring the cleanliness of the environment. She also made sure the soldiers received proper nutrition that would enable them to regain their health. She worked almost all hours of the day and made a habit of making her rounds even at night, carrying a lamp to light her way and provide comfort to ill and despairing soldiers.

Within six months, "The Lady of the Lamp" had succeeded in decreasing the death rate to 2.2 percent, thereby earning a deep respect for the profession of nursing.[37] C. Woodham-Smith, in his biography of Nightingale, wrote: "Two figures emerged from the Crimea as heroic, the soldier and the nurse."[38]

NURSING SCHOOLS

The Nightingale Training School for Nurses was established in 1860, a few years after the Crimean War ended. A year before that, Nightingale had published a book, *Notes on Nursing*, which became the standard text for nursing schools in England.[39] She emphasized that nursing was a challenging and important profession and that nurses were not to be confused with maids or servants: "A nurse should do nothing but nurse.... If you want a charwoman [a cleaning woman], have one. Nursing is a specialty."[40]

It was not long before this newfound respect for the nursing profession made its way across the Atlantic Ocean to the United States. One of the pillars of American nursing, however, was actually born in Germany in 1829— Marie E. Zakrzewska. As a girl, Zakrzewska used to assist her mother in midwifery duties and, at the age of 22, she became chief midwife and a professor at the midwifery school in a hospital in Berlin.[41]

In 1853, she sailed to the United States where she was determined to work in the medical field. She attended Cleveland Medical College, her tuition paid by an organization of women's rights advocates. Zakrzewska earned her medical degree in 1856, the same year Florence Nightingale returned to England from the Crimean War as a heroine.[42] Zakrzewska dreamed of opening and running a medical school and hospital that focused on the health needs of women and children exclusively. "In her view," wrote Stille, such a hospital would "aid in training women doctors and nurses while providing the best possible care for needy women and children."[43] After a few false starts and disappointments, "Dr. Zak," as she became known, worked with a group of Bostonian women and founded the New England Hospital of

Nursing and Religion

Florence Nightingale, like many of history's other first nurses, considered her profession to be a religious calling. In 1837, while still a young woman, she claimed to have heard God's voice calling her as she stood in the gardens of her family home. According to Nightingale, God called upon her to do his work although she did not understand at the time what that meant. Later, when she became immersed in the needs of the ill and wounded, she realized that her calling was to care for the sick. Mary Eliza Mahoney, who was also religious and had a strong faith in God, very likely believed her work was also a religious calling.

The relationship between these pioneer nurses and religion is not surprising. Most young women growing up in England and the United States in the 1800s had a religious education even if their schooling was not formal. Mahoney attended a public school in which moral instruction was heavily emphasized. Caring for the sick was viewed as charitable, humanitarian work that complemented what it meant to be a good Christian. Nursing was also a way to put one's faith into action and have a direct impact on the lives of the needy and downtrodden (although it may not have been deemed a proper pastime for women of elite social circles).

For Mahoney, however, the link between nursing and religion was even stronger because her childhood in Boston would have also exposed her to the strong tides of the abolitionist movement. Most white abolitionists were motivated by a religious tendency to reject hatred and discrimination and to respect all humankind equally. Perhaps for Mahoney, the interest in nursing was a natural one, the outgrowth of a general atmosphere in which religion and behavior were directly connected.

Women and Children. (For more on this hospital, enter "New England Hospital of Women and Children" into any search engine and browse the sites listed.)

HISTORY OF THE NEW ENGLAND HOSPITAL

The New England Hospital for Women and Children was founded in 1862—shortly after the outbreak of the Civil War—and began offering nursing courses one year later. It was the first American institution to offer formal and professional nursing training. Thanks to the efforts of Dr. Zak, the 1863 hospital charter provided for a nursing school. On June 5, 1863, the objectives of the hospital were announced:

I. To provide for women medical aid by competent physicians of their own sex.

II. To assist educated women in the practical study of medicine.

III. To train nurses for the care of the sick.[44]

The earliest students received a mere six months of training. Clearly, the program for training nurses was still in its infancy. The first women to complete the program received neither diplomas nor official certificates of any kind.[45] At first, the rate of enrollment was also quite slow; not many women applied to the program. Indeed, the hospital completed the training of only six nursing students in the first two years.

By 1878, when Mary Eliza Mahoney entered the program, it was already 16 years old. The intervening years had resulted in much improvement. By the time Mahoney enrolled, the program had been extended to one year. In the *American Journal of Nursing*, H.W. Munson cites a description of the specifics of the program:

Young women of suitable requirements and character will be admitted to the Hospital as school nurses for one year. This year will be divided into four periods; three months will be given respectively to the practical study of nursing in the Medical, Surgical, and Maternity Wards, and night nursing. Here the pupil will aid the head nurse in all the care and work of the wards under the direction of the Attending and Resident Physicians and Medical Students.[46]

It was also determined that "Certificates will be given to such nurses as have satisfactorily passed a year in practical training in the Hospital."[47] The first graduate of this new, formal program was Melinda Ann Richards, known as Linda Richards, who thus became the first academically trained American nurse. In her book on the history of nursing, Donahue noted that certification from a professional nursing program helped Richards' career tremendously, as "she was overwhelmed with job offers upon her graduation."[48]

The nurses and doctors who trained at the hospital were under Dr. Zak's strict supervision, and they received a thorough education. They were schooled in handling childbirth and battling contagious diseases like tuberculosis. They also regularly observed surgeries.[49]

PROGRESSIVE REPUTATION

Under Zak's direction, the hospital thrived and enjoyed an increasingly favorable reputation as a premier medical and nursing school. It also became known as quite a progressive institution. Years later, Helen Miller wrote, "Although Dr. Zakrzewska was considered to be an aristocrat, she preferred to be remembered as a woman willing to work for the advancement of all women. Could this desire have helped facilitate the admission of this 'first coloured girl' [on] March 23, 1878?"[50] The "coloured girl" in question was Mary Eliza Mahoney.

The hospital also earned a progressive reputation due to one of its physicians, Dr. Susan Dimock. Stringent about keeping educational standards high, Dimock believed in long, demanding training. After the success of Florence Nightingale and the recognition she earned for her work during the Crimean War, the entire field of nursing received a boost in respectability. Dimock and others wanted to ensure that a lack of rigorous training did not deflate that newfound level of respect with which society viewed the nursing profession.

RIGOROUS TRAINING

A sample day at the New England Hospital for Women and Children resembled the following:

> Nurses in those days arose at 5:30 A.M. and left the wards at 9:30 P.M. to retire to their beds, which were situated in little rooms between the wards. This meant that each nurse took care of her ward of six patients day and night, often not getting to sleep before the next call was heard.[51]

Susan Dimock added courses on surgical nursing to the curriculum, including "valuable information about the care used in the treatment of surgical cases as well as in minor accidents not requiring the attendance of a professional surgeon."[52] Her aim was to boost the status of nurses although there is some controversy about this issue. In an article about May Eliza Mahoney, Mary Ellen Doona, wrote, "Apparently the hospital's founding feminists were not without their blind spots. Instead of an inclusive sisterhood, there was a demarcation between the women who trained for nursing and those who studied medicine."[53] In other words, according to Doona, doctors in training at the New England Hospital were given top priority and special attention while nurses in training were used as a cheap "labor force."[54] Part of this distinction even lay in how the administration of the New England Hospital used different terms to refer to those who came to study at the institution: The nurses in training were referred to as "pupils" while the doctors in training were dubbed "students." Although the difference in terminology may seem minor, it contributed significantly to the way in which the nurses were viewed. The pupil nurses worked at the behest of the student doctors and were responsible for managing the daily events at the hospital and helping the doctors. In other words, a class system was established with the nurses at the bottom of the order and the doctors at the top.

SOCIAL CONCERNS

Dimock also became concerned about the high numbers of poor and homeless women who lacked proper maternity care in the Boston region. Many of the women were unmarried and were therefore spurned by society. Pregnancy without marriage was simply unacceptable. Dimock and others believed their job was to withhold moral judgment in order to provide objective, genuine care. They helped educate the women about the care of their children and even helped some of them to find employment in occupations where they could bring their children to work with them. The focus on the needs of single mothers by Dimock and her colleagues was unprecedented, and they worked in the hope that society at large would come to care about this often overlooked group of women.

In and around Boston, nursing was becoming an increasingly desirable profession, especially for young, working-class women. The legend of Florence Nightingale, the social prominence of women like Drs. Zakrzewska and Dimock, and the reputation of the New England Hospital all contributed to a new social attitude towards nursing. Many who had thought nurses fell into the same category as nannies, servants, and maids began to understand the profession. Nursing earned special prestige after the American Civil War, fought between 1861 and 1865, in which nurses proved to be an invaluable asset.

3 Nursing and the Civil War

CIVIL WAR HEROES

Because so little is known of Mahoney's life, it is unclear how her interest in nursing emerged. It can be surmised, however, that the role of nurses during the Civil War had a significant role to play in Mahoney's decision to pursue a career in nursing.

When the war erupted in 1861, there was neither an organized nursing force nor an ambulance service nor a medical team. The need for trained and organized medical personnel became clear almost immediately. Nuns from various religious denominations, who were accustomed to treating the ill and maimed, volunteered to treat injured and sick soldiers. They had the benefit of being already organized, and they were quickly able to fill the need for nurses during the Civil War's initial phase:

> Approximately six hundred Sisters from twelve orders participated during this critical period in history. They were given permission by President Abraham Lincoln to purchase any supplies needed for their work. Lincoln knew that most "good nursing" was being done by these religious sisterhoods, that they had helped in epidemics, that they were already organized and accustomed to discipline and obedience to authority. He therefore supported their efforts to the fullest.[55]

VOLUNTEER NURSES

Despite the sisters' hard work, this was not enough to handle the overwhelming number of casualties and wounded soldiers. Donahue reports that hundreds of men and women, all civilians, volunteered to care for the ill and injured. The numbers are not accurate, but "between two and ten thousand women or more were engaged in nursing and hospital administration during the Civil War." [56] Perhaps the prestige accorded these volunteer nurses was partly related to the celebrities among them. Walt Whitman, America's premier poet, was among the volunteers, as was Louisa May Alcott, the author of *Little Women*.[57] Stationed at a hospital in Washington D.C., in 1862, at the height of the war, Alcott kept a journal of her experiences:

> Up at six, dress by gaslight, run through my ward and throw up the windows, though the men grumble and shiver. But the air is bad enough to breed a pestilence, and as no notice is taken of our frequent appeals for better ventilation, I must do what I can ... for a more perfect pestilence box than this house I never saw—cold, damp, dirty, full of vile odors from wounds, kitchens, washrooms, stables. Till noon I trot, trot, trot, giving out rations, cutting up food for helpless 'boys,' washing faces, teaching my attendants how beds are made or floors are swept, dressing wounds, dusting tables, sewing bandages, keeping my tray tidy, rushing up and down after pillows, bed linens, sponges, and directions until it seems as if I would joyfully pay down all I possess for fifteen minutes rest. At twelve comes dinner for the patients and afterward there is letter writing for them or reading aloud. Supper at five sets everyone running that can run ... evening amusements ... then, for such as need them, the final doses for the night.[58]

In 1863, Alcott published a book about her experiences. It was entitled *Hospital Sketches* and became very popular as a detailed look at the suffering caused by the war.

Walt Whitman, like Alcott, followed his instinct as a writer and put his experiences to paper. His Civil War poems moved people by their detailed descriptions. In a poem entitled "The Wound-Dresser," he wrote:

> Bearing the bandages, water and sponge,
>
> Straight and swift to my wounded I go,
>
> Where they lie on the ground after the battle brought in,
>
> Where their priceless blood reddens the grass, the ground,
>
> Or to the rows of the hospital tent, or under the roof's hospital,
>
> To the long rows of cots up and down each side I return,
>
> To each and all one after another I draw near, not one do I miss,
>
> An attendant follows holding a tray, he carries a refuse pail,
>
> Soon to be fill'd with clotted rags and blood, emptied, and fill'd again.[59]

The image of the war portrayed by Walt Whitman was grisly and grim, hardly what a young woman of Mary Eliza Mahoney's age might imagine for herself as she considered a career. People like Whitman, however, despite their gruesome descriptions of the war, made the job of nursing seem heroic and patriotic. Indeed, the idea of devotion to a noble profession was inspirational and honorable, and many answered the call to duty. Some became famous.

INSPIRATIONS

One woman who became famous during the Civil War was Dorothea Lynde Dix.[60] Born in 1802, Dix was a schoolteacher and ran a school for several years, even turning down a promising marriage proposal in 1821 to devote her life to teaching. Her difficult work schedule eventually caused her to suffer a nervous breakdown in 1836, and this prompted her to take an extended vacation to England. When she returned to the United States in 1841, she was ready to begin a second career—treating the mentally ill. In Boston, she began teaching Sunday school classes for female inmates at the East Cambridge Jail. She noticed that several of the inmates suffered from mental illness but were being mistreated because most people understood very little about the mentally ill. Dix became an advocate for the rights of the mentally ill, and her work led to the establishment of dozens of hospitals for the care of such patients as well as to research on mental illness. Her prominence and dedication in this field led her to be called upon to serve as Superintendent of the Female Nurses of the Union Army in 1861.[61] (For more on Dorothea Dix, enter her name into any search engine and browse the sites listed.)

SOJOURNER TRUTH

Other famous volunteer nurses included Sojourner Truth, an African-American woman who, after being freed from slavery, became famous as a leader for African-American rights and women's rights. Born in New York in 1799 as Isabella Baumfree, she was a slave trained as a nurse. She was eventually sold by her owner to a family that was in need of a nurse's services. While she was working for this family, the state of New York passed an emancipation law, and Baumfree was set free in 1827. She moved to New York City shortly thereafter, and as author Althea T. Davis described, Baumfree "experienced a calling to travel (journey) and speak out against the injustices of slavery and women's equality (truth). A powerful orator with the gifts of voice and song and a commanding presence, she changed her name to Sojourner Truth."[62] At a meeting in Massachusetts, she officially joined the abolitionist movement and became a voice against slavery. Sojourner Truth also embraced feminist causes. In 1852, at the Women's Rights Convention in Akron, Ohio, she gave a speech that made her famous. One line that is attributed to her, even though there is no accurate copy remaining of that speech, was "Ain't I a woman?" The words were set to poetry by Erlene Stetson and are excerpted here:

"Ain't I a woman?

And ain't I a woman?

Look at me

Look at my arm!

I have plowed and planted

and gathered into barns

and no man could head me . . .

And ain't I a woman?

I could work as much

and eat as much as a man—

when I could get to it—

and bear the lash as well

and ain't I a woman?

I have born 13 children

and seen most all sold into slavery

and when I cried out a mother's grief

none but Jesus heard me . . .

. . . . If the first woman God ever made

was strong enough to turn the world

upside down, all alone

together women ought to be able to turn it

rightside up again"[63]

In 1850, William Garrison Lloyd's newspaper, *The Liberator*, published *The Narrative of Sojourner Truth*. Truth, who was illiterate, had dictated her biography to her neighbor. In 1863, Harriet Beecher Stowe published an essay, "Sojourner Truth, the Libyan Sibyl," in the *Atlantic Monthly*. The essay helped cement Truth's growing reputation as an important voice for women and slaves. Two years later, Sojourner Truth met with President Andrew Johnson to discuss the condition of freed slaves. Two years later, Sojourner Truth met with President Abraham Lincoln, who claimed to have heard of her travels and efforts before he reached the White House.

During the Civil War, Truth was assigned by the War Department to work at a hospital in Freedmen's Village, a town in northern Virginia that was built on a plantation seized by the Union army from Confederate general Robert E. Lee. This was seen as quite appropriate because General Lee represented the determination of the southern states to maintain the institution of slavery. In 1862, Congress passed a measure that liberated all slaves in Washington, D.C. These freed slaves fled to Freedmen's Village, the population of which swelled to several thousand.[64] The overpopulated town was soon beset by financial difficulties. Although she was almost 70 years old at the time, Sojourner Truth accepted the position in the hospital and performed her duties "to promote order, cleanliness, industry, and virtue among the patients."[65] Truth understood the value of a sanitary environment to good health. According to Althea T. Davis:

> Truth spent a great deal of time in Freedmen's Village caring for patients in the hospital. Cleanliness was a major thrust of her work and she organized a group of women to clean Freedmen's Hospital. Her philosophy was that the sick can never be made well in dirty surroundings. Truth's strong voice could be heard throughout the corridors: 'Be clean! Be clean!'[66]

After the war ended, Truth worked diligently to urge the U.S. Congress to fund the education of nurses and other medical personnel. At the time of her death, she had been working to resettle freed slaves from Freedmen's Village in the largely unsettled territories of the American West. She had even petitioned Congress to approve the use of federal land for this resettlement. Nell Irvin Painter describes Truth as "the principal symbol of strength and blackness in the iconography of women's culture."[67] Truth's prominence in the northeastern United States and her fame within the African-American community no doubt made her a known and familiar figure to Mary Eliza Mahoney.

HARRIET TUBMAN

Mahoney certainly had other African-American female role models in the nursing profession. One was Harriet Tubman, also a major figure in the movement to abolish slavery. Known as the "Moses of her people" for her efforts in leading slaves to freedom by way of the Underground Railroad, Tubman became a nurse or "matron" at a Virginia hospital where African-American soldiers were treated during the Civil War. In the 1890s, Tubman was honored at a party in Boston that the New England Women's Suffrage Association had organized to recognize her efforts and achievements.[68]

It is important to note that, while women like Sojourner Truth and Harriet Tubman supported women's rights, their first priority was the abolition of slavery and the advancement of African Americans. "Racial equality was the first order of business for black women abolitionists, and the movement for women's rights was a close second," noted Althea T. Davis.[69] One way for African Americans to advance was to enter a profession like nursing. Truth and Tubman "represent the era of the untrained nurse who, in addition to nursing, chose to become actively involved in eradicating the social injustices of slavery and the inequality of women in American society."[70]

The fact that two famous and widely respected African-American women had lent their names and efforts to the worthy cause of nursing was no doubt known to Mahoney, who was 20 when the Civil War ended. Nursing, of course, was not yet an established profession in the United States, but it was a worthy cause to which many women devoted their lives. The profession had not yet been formalized or standardized in the United States, especially where African-American women were concerned, but times were changing.

MAHONEY ENROLLS

When she first began working at the New England Hospital for Women and Children, Mary Eliza Mahoney was not a student but a washerwoman and a laundress. She performed this work for some time before making a decision to apply to the nursing program.

It is interesting to consider her application to the nursing program in the light of her personal life. Most women in the

Harriet Tubman

Without a doubt, Harriet Tubman was one of the most remarkable women of America's Civil War era. In gauging the men and women who probably had an impact on the life of Mary Eliza Mahoney, it is certain that Tubman's story would have had much influence.

Born Harriet Ross in 1820 in Maryland, she grew up as a slave. Both of her parents were also slaves, and their white master treated his slaves with extreme brutality. Tubman suffered whippings and beatings regularly as a child. At the age of 12, she witnessed her master punishing a slave who had tried to escape. When he ordered Tubman to help him tie up the captured runaway, she refused and was beaten so severely that she suffered a serious head injury.*

When she was 25, she married John Tubman, who was a free African American. Harriet Tubman knew her marriage would be in jeopardy should she be sold, because many couples were often torn apart when one spouse was sold and sent to live elsewhere. At the age of 30, she realized there late 1800s who sought a professional career, as opposed to what can be considered ordinary employment, were unmarried. They had to support themselves financially and planned to live independent lives. Mahoney had worked as a private nurse for several families before working as a washer, maid, and cook at the hospital. She was earning a living to help her family, and one might wonder why she chose to pursue a professional career in nursing. The sudden prominence nursing gained during the Civil War is one answer; an additional answer may lie in Mahoney's personal life.

In researching Mahoney's biography, Helen Miller interviewed Mahoney's descendants. They informed her that Mahoney had had a suitor at one time and that she "had

was a real chance that she would indeed be sold and sent to the southern states. This prompted her to act, and she plotted her escape.

With the help of some sympathetic white farmers, Tubman made her escape north where she received further assistance from the Philadelphia Anti-slavery Society. In Philadelphia, Tubman learned about the unique and complex system known as the Underground Railroad, a secret route by which slaves were aided in escaping to the northern states.**

Before long, Tubman became one of the best-known names associated with the Underground Railroad, helping more than 300 slaves find freedom. She was known and admired for her personal fortitude, her religious faith, and her willingness to improve the lives of fellow African Americans.***

* "The Life of Harriet Tubman," New York History Net, *http://www.nyhistory. com/harriettubman/life.htm*. (Retrieved February 19, 2004).

** Ibid.

*** Ibid.

prepared a hope chest after the engagement was announced to a physician."[71] It is unclear how old Mahoney was at the time of her engagement to this unnamed doctor, but it is reasonable to assume—given the young age at which women married in the 1800s—that she was in her late teens or early 20s.

Mahoney's engagement did not last. The physician, according to Mahoney's descendants, "later jilted her and she remained very bitter for several years."[72] Such an experience would have hurt anyone, but Mahoney's emotions seem to have been especially damaged. She never married, deciding to remain single all her life. It may be assumed that she chose to enter the nursing profession in order to sustain her independence, that she chose a career so that she would never have to depend on a man to support her. In this, she can be compared to Florence Nightingale who also chose to be married only to her profession.

ATYPICAL APPLICANT

At the age of 33, Mahoney was older than the typical applicant to nursing school. It is unknown what took her so long to apply to the nursing program at the New England Hospital for Women and Children, but race and finances were probably the dual culprits. The hospital's admission standards were not very open, and tuition was expensive. As noted above, Mahoney had previously worked as a nurse for prominent families in Boston. Although she had first-hand experience in the nursing field, it is safe to say that nurses without professional training still had to contend with situations in which they were expected to perform duties that maids usually did—laundry, cleaning, and food preparation. Perhaps her work as an untrained nurse made her aspire to something better.

The New England Hospital had yet to admit a woman of color into its doctoral or its nursing program, and it is therefore interesting to speculate why it admitted Mary Eliza Mahoney in 1878. It has been suggested that a Mrs. Ednah Dow Cheney, who served in various capacities of the hospital, had a hand in the decision to admit Mahoney. Having served as manager, president, and secretary for the hospital, Cheney had a great deal of influence with the hospital's other administrators. She was also known for her belief in what is today called equal opportunity employment: "In choosing among applicants," she said, "fitness should be the only test. Religious belief, color, nationality, must never enter into the decision."[73]

Cheney had several prominent African-American friends, including Harriet Tubman and Booker T. Washington, and it is likely that she may have encouraged the hospital's administrators to start accepting African-American students. In 1878, the hospital admitted Caroline Still, a young African-American woman, as an intern. Later that year, 13 years after the end of the Civil War, Mary Eliza Mahoney became the first African-American woman to be accepted to a professional nursing program.[74]

BREAKING THE COLOR LINES

Admitting Mahoney was a very radical and progressive step for the New England Hospital even though the founders had all been women and one might imagine they would be receptive to the idea of tearing down barriers. As Donahue noted, however, "As in most Northern schools, racial quotas had been established at the New England Hospital; the charter of the nursing school allowed for only *one* Negro and *one* Jewish student to be accepted each year."[75] Although some of the hospital administrators were trying to change the status quo, the hospital had a long way to go. One positive step along this path was admitting Mary Eliza Mahoney to the nursing program. Mahoney's role in this decision cannot be overlooked. As Miller observed, "Miss Mahoney had the moral courage to venture out in a profession where no black had ever attempted."[76]

The timing of Mahoney's arrival at the New England Hospital in 1878 was also curious. Susan Dimock, the medical professor at the Hospital who had been responsible for revolutionizing the curriculum, had died three years before Mahoney arrived. According to Doona, "While traveling on a European vacation, the twenty-eight-year-old doctor was swept overboard and drowned when her fog-enshrouded ship struck rocks at the Scilly Islands." She added, "It is reasonable to assume that the little hospital still felt the painful loss of their most promising doctor."[77]

The loss of Dimock was compounded by some difficult financial times for the New England Hospital. In 1872, a fire in the city of Boston had rocked the economy, threatening to collapse it. Many institutions and companies faced a dire financial outlook, and the nurses at the New England Hospital even began donating one-quarter of their earnings to the hospital to maintain it.[78] The future seemed unsteady indeed.

Scenes from the Life of Mary Eliza Mahoney

Florence Nightingale, first to develop a training program for nurses in Britain, during the Crimean War, in the 1850s. Nightingale's strict tradition of nurses' training carried over to several American nursing schools, including Massachusetts General Hospital in Boston, Bellevue Hospital in New York, and the New Haven Hospital in Connecticut.

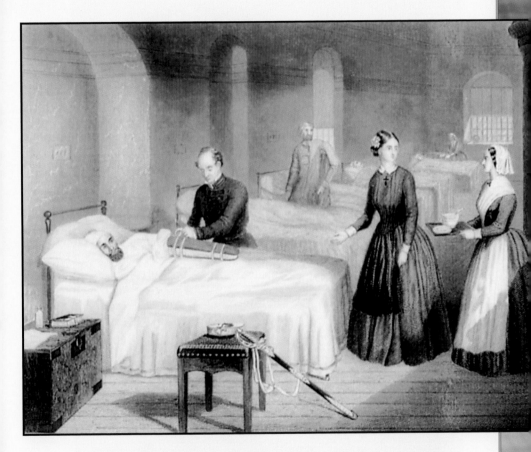

A drawing showing Florence Nightingale at the hospital at Scutari, during the Crimean War. Nightingale managed the hospital there and developed a program to train nurses. By improving sanitary conditions, she drastically reduced the mortality rate at the hospital, saving many lives. After the war, Nightingale returned home to found a training program for nurses, which served as a template for nurses training programs worldwide.

Dorothea Dix (1802–1887), teacher and advocate for the mentally ill. Dix traveled through the country, making recommendations to local and state governments on improving treatment of the insane. When the Civil War broke out, Dix volunteered to organize a nurses' corps, and she was made Superintendent of Nurses for the Union Army.

Frances Payne Bolton, philanthropist and long-time member of the U.S. House of Representatives. Bolton helped underwrite expenses of the young National Association of Colored Graduate Nurses (NACGN) during its fight for integration. As a young woman, Bolton accompanied members of the Visiting Nurses Association on their rounds in poor neighborhoods; this sparked her life-long interest in the nursing profession.

Adah Belle Samuels Thoms (1870–1943), an early advocate for the National Association of Colored Graduate Nurses (NACGN), invited Martha Franklin, the association's founder, to hold the association's first meeting in New York, under the sponsorship of the Lincoln Hospital Alumnae Assocation, of which she was president. Thoms served as first treasurer of NACGN and was later elected president. She was the first recipient of the Mary Mahoney Award of the NACGN. This award was later adopted by the American Nurses Association, when the two assocations merged.

The NACGN, founded on August 25, 1908 to promote the standards and welfare of black nurses and to break down racial discrimination in the profession. The organization held its first convention in Boston in 1919 (shown). Mary Eliza Mahoney, the first black American trained nurse, addressed the convention. The association awarded her life membership in 1911 and elected her its national chaplain.

Three nurses in a lounge at the Colored Home and Hospital, New York City, 1910. The hospital was originally founded by philanthropists to care for lower-income New Yorkers, especially African Americans, but it eventually became a general hospital open to all people regardless of race. The hospital's name was changed to Lincoln Hospital, after the Great Emancipator. Its nursing program, formed in response to nationwide racial discrimination in nursing education in the 1890s, was one of the best in the country, and its graduates enjoyed its excellent reputation.

WANTED
MORE NAVY NURSES
Be a commissioned officer in the U.S. Navy

Phyllis Mae Daley, the first black Navy nurse, with several other newly commissioned nurses. The induction of black nurses into the Navy, the result of a telegram campaign and other behind-the-scenes work orchestrated by Mabel Staupers, NACGN executive secretary, came on the heels of the announcement of the shortage of qualified nurses in the armed forces and the possibility of a draft. Black nurses, women's groups, and sympathetic white allies across the country rose up, protesting the unfairness of instituting a draft, while willing black nurses were being turned away.

Sojourner Truth, born Isabella Baumfree, a former slave and traveling preacher, was among the first to spread abolition and women's rights activism, and to link the two. Truth sometimes moved her audiences to tears with her heart-wrenching stories of what it was like to be a slave. She was a much-sought-after speaker because of her moving oratories on human rights.

American Red Cross club director Harvey Shaw, of Philadelphia, pours coffee for U.S. Army nurses and officers serving in the Southwest Pacific (specifically, in Australia), on March 11, 1944. The black officers were from Illinois, Ohio, Michigan, Missouri, and New York.

Commander Thomas A. Gaylor of the U.S. Navy, administering oath to five new Navy nurses commissioned in New York in 1945. Phyllis Mae Dailey (second from right), a graduate of Lincoln School for Nurses, became the first of four black nurses sworn into the Navy Nurse Corps as an ensign.

Mary Eliza Mahoney's gravesite, in Woodlawn Cemetery, Everett,
Massachusetts. When Helen S. Miller, an African-American nurse who
had become interested in Mahoney's life, found the site in 1969, it was
overgrown with weeds and the cement marker lay below the grass surface.
Miller, appalled at the grave's obvious neglect, contacted Chi Eta Phi Sorority,
a sorority of African-American registered nurses to which she belonged, as
well as the American Nurses Association to help with a project to honor
Mahoney, on August 15, 1973, Mahoney's new gravesite was unveiled. The
stone carries a likeness of Mahoney and the words "The First Professional
Negro Nurse in the U.S.A."

4 Something
to Prove

MAHONEY THE STUDENT

When Mahoney entered the one-year program at the New England Hospital in 1878, she was one of 40 students to be admitted that year. Applicants were required to be "well and strong, between the ages of 21 and 31, and have a good reputation as to character and disposition."[79] Mahoney, of course, was 33—two years older than the maximum age requirement. This seems to have been overlooked, perhaps because she was known to the administration through her previous employment at the hospital as a maid, cook, and washerwoman.

Of the 40 women who applied that year, only 18 were accepted for a trial period.[80] During this probationary period, the nursing students took courses and worked at the bedsides of patients. The rigor of this period gave the students a sense of what they could expect for the next year. After the trial period, only half of the 18 were kept on for the program; of those 9, only 3 made it to graduation and earned their nursing diplomas.

The rigor of the program, as well as the "sheer physical endurance,"[81] contributed to the dwindling numbers. The students worked long hours, from 5:30 A.M. to 9:30 P.M. each day. They were paid according to one of the tenets of the program: "In order to enable women entirely dependent upon their work for support to obtain a thorough training, the nurses will be paid for their work from one to four dollars per week after the first fortnight, according to the actual value of their service to the Hospital."[82] The wages did not amount to anything substantial, especially when, as mentioned earlier, most nurses returned 25 percent to the hospital to help it through its financial difficulties. Students were also expected to pay for their uniforms, which were "simple calico dresses" and "felt slippers."[83]

While in the program, Mahoney, like other nurses, was charged with caring for an entire ward in the hospital;

each ward consisted of six beds.[84] There is some evidence that the hospital used nursing students like Mahoney as inexpensive labor rather than students. As Doona noted, though students did not pay tuition, "much of the training was evidently more service than education."[85] Other writers, like Darlene Stille, disagreed, saying that the founders of the New England Hospital for Women and Children were all women who would not exploit other women. "The pioneering medical women who founded the hospital," she wrote, "had suffered a great deal of discrimination in their struggle to become doctors, so they were sympathetic to a young, bright, black woman wanting to become a nurse."[86] This does not explain why it took nearly 16 years for the hospital to admit an African-American woman into its program. Doona described what little is known of Mahoney's performance during her studies:

> She endured the rigors of the program in spite of her diminutive stature. She was less than five feet tall and weighed under one hundred pounds. Evidently, this little woman had more than met the admission requirements as a student with 'robust health.' In spite of the infectious diseases prevalent during that era, she did not miss one day, although frequently her classmates did.[87]

Perhaps Mahoney felt that, because of her race, the hospital administration expected less of her than of her classmates. It cannot be doubted that Mahoney felt pressure to excel because of her position as the first and only African-American student in the nursing program. Her hard work, as has Helen Miller suggested, probably led to one very positive result: "The New England Hospital School continued to accept Negro students whenever applicants met the required qualification."[88] Mahoney's own sister later applied to the program and was accepted. Mahoney had paved the way for her and scores of others.

A NURSING CAREER

Mahoney graduated on August 1, 1879, having completed the program in one year. She was among the approximately 13 percent of the original 40 applicants to actually complete the training program. The program director said of the graduates, "It is believed that [they] are fully entitled to confidence as efficient nurses and will be sure not to disappoint those who may employ them."[89] Although some of the nurses certainly went on to prominent and successful careers, Mary Mahoney's post-graduate work has not been documented.

Most of the graduates went to work for families in private settings and were not employed by the large public hospitals. The larger hospitals did not seem to have a need for nurses when they used student nurses to do most of the labor in return for minimum wages. A 1923 Goldmark study revealed "how students, promised an education, would be used instead as a labor force. This practice prevented the growth of the profession, for it eliminated the necessary imaginative consideration of learning between practitioners and novices."[90]

Nevertheless, this seemingly common practice of using student nurses rather than hiring fully trained graduates resulted in Mahoney's establishing her own practice. Because many African-American nurses had trouble finding employment in major, well-funded hospitals and because black hospitals rarely paid adequate salaries, they entered private practice. It is feasible that Mahoney's 40 years of private practice were largely the result of rejections by white hospitals. She made her niche in caring for pregnant women and new mothers and their newborn babies. Much of her work was centered in New Jersey, but she once traveled to Washington to care for the husband of a friend. The man, an army surgeon, had contracted tuberculosis, and when it was clear that his illness was fatal, she accompanied him to North Carolina.[91] Her patients benefited from her loyalty and generous nature, as well as her intelligence and compassion.

Miller described the gratitude of the Armes family to Mahoney: "Mr. Armes said of her, 'I owe my life to that dear soul.'"[92] Indeed, a New England Hospital staff member, a

Social Attitudes Towards Nursing

Today's nurses are professionally trained men and women whose contributions to the medical field are appreciated and recognized. Before Florence Nightingale revolutionized the profession, however, nursing was not deemed a profession at all. It was considered by many not even a worthwhile activity.

Before the 1800s, nursing was a chore performed by women and men—though usually women—in religious orders, especially Catholic nuns. The sisters typically traveled to war zones or battle sites, caring for wounded soldiers and innocent civilians caught in the crossfire. They also tended to the ill on a local level, setting up impromptu hospitals in urban centers and slums.

Because most people who sought hospital care were those who could not afford private care at home, hospitals were often considered to be poorhouses, and not much was done to improve their condition. Because conditions in these hospitals were unsanitary, disease spread easily. According to Evelyn Carruthers, since "proper" young women would not risk their reputations by volunteering at contemporary of Mahoney's, said, "I used to hear her praises sung everywhere around Boston and suburbs."[93]

PRIVATE LIFE

The life of a private practice nurse was very difficult. Nurses lived with the families for whom they cared. Unfortunately, and this was especially true for African-American nurses; they were also treated like servants rather than trained professionals. Mary Eliza Mahoney attempted to instill changes in the role of the private nurse on an individual as well as an organizational basis.

a hospital, "those who provided nursing care were commonly persons who had been imprisoned for drunkenness or who could not find work elsewhere."*

So when did nursing start to become a respectable profession, suitable for "proper" young women and others who were interested? A change took place after the Crimean War when Nightingale proved nursing's effectiveness. Nightingale and other pioneers set the standards for nurses and for the field of nursing, demanding that nurses be trained thoroughly and be paid fairly for their services. In 1928, May Ayres Burgess wrote, "Nurses do love nursing, but they want nursing to be, in so far as possible, a profession, and the things they stress when they talk about the economic conditions under which they work ... are those things which other professional workers take for granted: Reasonable hours, Adequate income, Constructive leadership, [and] Opportunity for growth."**

* *Microsoft® Encarta® Online Encyclopedia 2004*, s.v. "Nursing," (by Evelyn Carruthers), http://encarta.msn.com

** May Ayres Burgess, *Nurses, Patients and Pocketbooks* (1928), p. 482.

It seems that Mahoney, at the beginning of her career, did as her employees requested, performing domestic duties in addition to her demanding nursing duties. Later in her career, she began to draw a fine line between the two sets of responsibilities: "One way of distinguishing herself in protest was by refusing to eat in the kitchen with the household help, separating herself and choosing to eat alone.... Mahoney also indicated on her reference that she would eat in the kitchen *alone*."[94]

Mahoney also chose to live alone. She lived in a small apartment in Warwick Street, in Roxbury. She spent her little free time participating in church activities with her sister. Her relatives reported that she enjoyed spending time alone, relaxing, and reading.

ONE MORE CHALLENGE

In the mid-1920s, Mahoney developed breast cancer; the tumor eventually metastasized, spreading from one part of her body to other parts. She entered the New England Hospital on December 7, 1926, on a free bed since her funds had apparently run out.[95] Now 81 years old, she was described by the doctors who attended to her as a "small, poorly nourished, colored woman. She was irrational and unable to give a history of her condition."[96] She had apparently been avoiding checking into a hospital; the developing cancer had been causing her to suffer for years and was depleting her finances. Upon entering the New England Hospital where she had been a nurse in training 50 years earlier, she was helped with her bills by the Family Welfare Society.[97]

Mahoney's cancer had advanced too far to be successfully treated, and she did not survive this latest challenge in her life. She passed away on January 4, 1926,[98] and was buried in the Woodlawn Cemetery, in Everett, Massachusetts, where she had previously purchased a grave lot.[99]

Mary Eliza Mahoney represented a wealth of possibilities for other aspiring and practicing African-American nurses. As the first African-American woman to earn a professional training certification in nursing, she demonstrated that the work itself was not the only challenge. Contrary to what many people of the time thought about the intelligence of African Americans, she also demonstrated that an African American could competently handle, and even excel in, the demands of the field. Her career proved that the only obstacle was society's biased and misinformed perspective of the abilities of African-American women and of African Americans as a whole.

REMEMBERING MARY ELIZA MAHONEY

Buried in the Woodlawn Cemetery in a quiet Boston suburb, Mahoney was largely forgotten for many years. That changed when Helen S. Miller, an African-American nurse, became interested in the life and legacy of Mary Eliza Mahoney. Miller began researching the life of Mahoney in the late 1960s, and she was dismayed to discover that there was almost no trace in history books of the first African-American nurse in the nation. She resolved to change this and began a major research project on Mahoney's life.

Miller tried to read as much as she could about Mahoney; she was shocked to find that very little had been written about her life. She then thought to try and find Mahoney's descendants, and here she met with some success. Although Mahoney had never married and had no children, Miller found the families of Mahoney's nieces and nephews still living in the Massachusetts area. She visited these family members several times and in 1969, one of Mahoney's great-nephews accompanied Miller to Mahoney's gravesite at the Woodlawn Cemetery. The condition in which they found the grave, however, indicated just how neglected Mahoney's life story had been. Miller described the event:

> We did not receive encouraging news from the office personnel at the cemetery. They gave us a map showing the section where the grave was. They informed us that the particular section had no headstones and it would be virtually impossible to locate a grave. Grass had grown all over the area and except for identification of the section by the map we were given, you could not hope to locate a grave. The flat cement marker was sunken deeply beneath the soil. We had to find it to identify the numbers 2674, which was listed in the office as that of Mary Eliza Mahoney. The members of Miss Mahoney's family and I began the awesome task of unearthing sections of the ground for several hours without success. Just as we were about to give up, we found Mary Mahoney's grave and also that of her brother and sister. We were overjoyed and thrilled that our mission did not end in vain. And yet, tears came to my eyes to think of this dear soul, who had given so much of her life to humanity and to the profession of nursing was forgotten after death.[100]

Miller recalled reading about how Mahoney, once she had established her private nursing practice, had often donated money, to her friends and others who were in need, to cover the cost of buying graves. It seemed ironic that Mahoney's own gravesite was a neglected ruin.

RESTORATION OF THE GRAVESITE

Helen Miller devised a plan to restore Mahoney's gravesite as well as pay tribute to her life achievements. It is possible that Miller, an African-American nurse, also wanted to reclaim the history of those who came before, and there was no better place to excavate the lost history than to begin with the history of the first professional African-American nurse.

Miller contacted the Chi Eta Phi Sorority, a sorority of African-American registered nurses to which she belonged, as well as the American Nurses Association. Plans were designed and implemented. On August 15, 1973, the unveiling of Mahoney's new gravesite was held in Everett, Massachusetts. As Miller noted, "It was a rainy day and we all got wet but the purpose of our being there brought sunshine to our hearts." [101]

The new monument marking Mahoney's grave was fashioned from granite stone and prominently featured a handcarved bust of Mahoney inscribed with the words "The United States First Professional Negro Nurse." Dignitaries present at the unveiling included members of the American Nursing Association's Board of Directors, the leadership of the Chi Eta Phi Sorority, and officials from the Massachusetts Nurses' Association, family and friends of Mary Mahoney, and D. DiBona, the sculptor of the monument. [102]

HONORING MAHONEY'S LEGACY

During the ceremony, several people spoke about the legacy of Mary Eliza Mahoney and of how her example had inspired generations of African-American nurses across the country. The speech delivered by Helen Miller on that day said it best:

> Our gathering here today is an occasion that is both unique and historical. It is unique in that the date August 15 is commemorated in Catholic Churches as the Feast of the Assumption of The Blessed Virgin Mary, as festal day in her honor. It is historical in the fact that this is the restored grave of the First Black Professional Nurse in the United States. To my knowledge, only two other Black Women of national fame have been

recorded a similar honor, that of having their graves restored years after burial: Sojourner Truth, the Great Emancipator whose grave is in Battle Creek, Michigan and Mary McLeod Bethune, the Great Educator and Humanitarian whose grave is located on the grounds of Bethune Cookman College, Daytona Beach, Florida. Neither of these graves however have sculptured on the marker the head of the deceased. It is significant then that two national nursing organizations have joined with others who are working toward the long overdue public recognition of this our First Nurse, to accord her the place in History she so richly deserves. When the family of Mary Mahoney accompanied me to this spot in 1968 we found a grass covered flat cement marker sunken beneath the soil and the inscription was only visible after scrapping and rubbing to identify the name and lot number that had been given to us by the cemetery personnel. In the days following this visit, I shared what had been found with my Sorority and with Anne Warner, former Director of Public Relations, ANA, enlisting their support in restoring Miss Mahoney's grave. I am overjoyed that both organizations supported the request which is evident as we unveil the lovely work of art to stand forever in memoriam to our First Professional Nurse.[103]

Helen Miller's efforts to revive interest in the life and work of Mary Eliza Mahoney did not stop at the restoration of her grave and the erection of a memorial. She also worked diligently to have Mahoney's life remembered in other ways. She sent letters to the Citizens Stamp Advisory Committee of the United States Post Office and to friends and colleagues in the nursing community who would be able to write their own letters in support of the idea. "We must not let the name Mary Mahoney pass into oblivion," she wrote. "It must be kept alive in as many ways as possible and the Commemorative Stamp can do this on a local, state, national and international level as no other medium can." [104] Support for the commemorative stamp continues, though it has yet to be issued.

The work of Helen Miller and other African-American nurses in the 1960s ensured that the memory of Mary Eliza Mahoney would not be forgotten. It is also important to trace her influence in the development of the nursing field and on the role African-American women played in it during the years after Mahoney's death. In the following chapters, we will explore and discuss this legacy of influence.

5

The National Association of Colored Graduate Nurses

THE BIRTH OF THE NACGN

The life—and the death—of Mary Eliza Mahoney were marked by her characteristic quiet attitude. Despite her quiet manner and preference for privacy, however, Mahoney helped to inspire and encourage a new generation of African-American women to enter and change the field of nursing forever. Her influence and legacy in the development of African-American women in nursing can be traced through the archives of nursing organizations, especially the National Association of Colored Graduate Nurses (NACGN).

MARTHA MINERVA FRANKLIN

As the first trained African-American nurse in the United States, Mary Eliza Mahoney understood that she had a role to play in the future of African Americans in the field. She became active in helping other African-American women achieve success in the nursing field, and she put her effort and energy behind an emerging organization called the National Association of Colored Graduate Nurses (NACGN).

The NACGN grew out of the imagination of Martha Minerva Franklin. By the late 1800s, several major hospitals and universities in the United States had established nursing schools. One of the better known and most prestigious was the Women's Hospital Training School for Nurses, which was located in Philadelphia, Pennsylvania. A native of Connecticut, Martha Minerva Franklin traveled to Philadelphia in the late 1890s to complete her nursing education at this institution. She graduated with her training credentials in 1897, the only African American in her graduating class. Franklin returned to Connecticut and took the state registration examination for nursing. She passed the examination in 1908—one of the first nurses in Connecticut to do so.[105]

As she began her professional career as a nurse, Franklin applied herself to the task of eliminating discrimination. Indeed, almost as soon as Mary Eliza Mahoney opened the doors for African-American women to enter the field, racism set in and distorted the mission of nursing. Many nursing schools began banning African-American students, and the number of rejected applications of qualified women made it necessary to open schools devoted exclusively to the nursing education of African-American women. The first of these, Spelman Seminary, opened its doors in 1886. Located in Atlanta, Georgia, it provided a model for other schools that were to follow in the early 1890s, including Hampton Institute (Virginia), Provident Hospital (Chicago), and Tuskegee Institute (Alabama). According to Donahue, "These schools experienced difficulties similar to those of the early white schools, but also suffered from societal prejudice toward blacks."[106]

NEED FOR NURSES

The Spanish American War, like all wars, underscored the need for a professional nursing corps to serve in the military and care for wounded and ill soldiers. Having a professional, well-trained corps of nurses greatly reduced the number of casualties and lifted troop morale. African-American nurses, however, were mistreated despite their willingness to serve their country.

When the war broke out in 1898, some of the primary medical concerns were the vicious outbreaks of typhoid and yellow fever, which caused approximately 75 percent of the deaths in the war.[107] The most prized nurses were those who were already immune to these diseases. African-American nurses soon became involved:

> On July 13, 1898, Namahyoke Curtis (wife of Dr. Austin Curtis, Superintendent of the Freedman's Hospital in Washington, D.C.) was asked to recruit immune nurses. Herself under contract to the Army as an immune nurse, Mrs. Curtis hired 32 black women who were allegedly immune to yellow fever. Most of her recruits went to

Santiago, Cuba, in July and August 1898, to serve in the worst of the epidemics. At least two of their number, T.R. Bradford and Minerva Trumbull, died from typhoid fever.[108]

It became clear that "immunity" was a concept not exempt from racism. According to Jacqueline Hodge, "Many black female volunteer nurses were told that they were immune to the diseases because their skin was darker and thicker. Because of this, many of them exposed themselves to the diseases and became casualties when they returned home."[109] Although little else has been found to substantiate this claim, it is not an unthinkable scenario given the many stereotypes that existed at the time.

TAKING ACTION

Franklin decided to take action. According to "Etched in Stone," "In 1906 and 1907, she surveyed nurses, directors of nursing schools, and nursing organizations to learn the numbers of black nurses in America and the extent of employment discrimination." She sent more than 500 letters to leaders in the nursing profession—including graduate nurses—to the boards of various nursing organizations, and to the heads of nursing schools.[110] Though it took her two years, and though some of her letters went unanswered, Franklin succeeded in putting her finger on the pulse of attitudes about race in the nursing profession.

She needed evidence to validate her suspicion that African-American women faced obstacles that their white counterparts did not. The evidence she gathered was apparently sufficient because she acted quickly to try to improve the situation for African-American women. According to Davis, "She realized that if this help were to materialize and be effective, it must be initiated by black nurses themselves. She believed that only through collective action could their problems be identified, analyzed, and thus eliminated."[111]

In 1908, one year after conducting her survey, Franklin led efforts to hold a conference of 52 graduate nurses in New York City. She won the support of the Lincoln School for Nurses Alumnae Association, which agreed to sponsor the meeting. The assistant superintendent of nurses and the acting director of the nursing program at the Lincoln Hospital School at the time was Adah Belle Samuels Thoms, a registered nurse who would later play a major role in the NACGN. Upon learning of Franklin's idea for establishing an organization for African-American nurses, Thoms demonstrated her support for it, believing in the goodness and potential success of the cause. She invited Franklin to hold the meeting in New York City.

Harlem, New York

When Adah Belle Samuels Thoms moved to New York City in 1893 to pursue her dream of becoming a nurse, she lived in Harlem, a neighborhood located on the northwestern side of the Manhattan island. It was a fortuitous move, as Harlem has long played a significant role in African-American history and cultural life. It has nourished the progress of the African-American community in the United States and continues to do so today.

The neighborhood was established in the mid-1600s by Dutch settlers. For 200 years, it remained a farming area, featuring the wealthy estates of New York's elite. In the late 1800s, when railroad tracks were laid down across the island, Harlem became accessible to other New Yorkers. The neighborhood sprang to life as a cultural center of Manhattan. People thronged to its opera house, its lively theater life, and its recreational events.*

The real estate market suffered in the early 1900s, and owners of new apartment complexes found no willing tenants.

ADAH BELLE SAMUELS THOMS

The life of Adah Belle Samuels Thoms before she met and began working with Franklin is one marked by significant achievement. She wrote a book entitled *Pathfinders: A History of the Progress of Colored Graduate Nurses*, which later became one of the key texts and sources of information about the role African-American women played in the emergence of the nursing profession. Thoms played one of the most pivotal roles in helping African-American nurses advance.

The year of her birth is uncertain, but it is estimated that Thoms was born in Richmond, Virginia, in 1870. She attended public schools in Richmond, and hoped to become a teacher. She even attended the Richmond Normal school, a two-year

To fill their spaces, they opened the rental market in Harlem to African Americans, many of whom had recently left the southern states and were looking to settle in the North. African Americans started flowing into Harlem, setting up homes, churches, cultural centers, and schools. Before long, Harlem became known as a primarily African-American neighborhood.**

History books best remember it as the site of the Harlem Renaissance, an era between 1920 and 1930 that saw African-American writers, singers, musicians, and artists explode onto the American cultural scene. Although the stock market crash of 1929 threw Harlem into a downward spiral, resulting in unemployment and poverty, the neighborhood always retained its cultural legacy and has experienced a revival in the last several years.

* "Harlem History," *http://www.harlemspirituals.com/harlem.html* (Retrieved February 20, 2004).

** Ibid.

school known for producing teachers and the only black teacher preparatory school in the region. After she completed the two-year program, she taught school in Richmond for a short time before becoming interested in nursing.[112]

PURSUING A CAREER

In 1893, at the age of 23, Thoms moved to New York City where African Americans had better opportunities for advancement than they had in the southern states where segregation and racism were practiced more intensely than in the North. Jim Crow laws and other racist laws had made opportunities for African Americans in the post-Civil War South very difficult. Historically, in the fields of medicine and nursing, African-American universities and colleges were graduating exceptional students, but those students found little employment opportunity in the South. They also had an impossible time getting political representation to advocate their cause.

Thoms moved to Harlem, a predominantly African-American neighborhood of New York. She enrolled in a nursing course at the Woman's Infirmary and School of Therapeutic Massage, which was not a formal program and did not even offer any sort of certification or credentials upon completion. According to Davis, "Historically, the ANA and the American Hospital Association recommended short courses of training in nursing to women who were not qualified by varied criteria for the full course, or who chose not to take the full course."[113] In addition to elementary science and biology, these short courses, such as the one offered by the Woman's Infirmary and School of Therapeutic Massage, included lessons to which Florence Nightingale and Mary Eliza Mahoney may have vehemently objected: cleaning, cooking, and household care.[114] Indeed, these courses seemed more suitable for women who wanted basic lessons in how to care for their families rather than for women who wanted to get an in-depth education in the nursing field.

Thoms became more deeply interested in the field of nursing and decided to pursue it seriously as a career. With this decision came the realization that the informal courses she was taking at the Woman's Infirmary and School of Therapeutic Massage were not going to help her advance her goals. According to Davis, "Thoms's evolving experience at this point could be comparable to the mid-twentieth century and present-day experience of women who enter practical nursing programs. They soon find their knowledge, skills, and/or scope of their practice limited, relevant to their aspirations in nursing, and decide to continue their education."[115]

LINCOLN HOSPITAL AND HOME

In 1903, Thoms entered the Lincoln Hospital and Home, a hospital that dated back to 1839. It was originally established by a group of wealthy white philanthropists to serve the medical needs of those New Yorkers who could not afford health care and who fell in the lower economic ranks of society, especially African Americans. Indeed, it was first named the Home for the Relief of Aged Indigent Black Persons. In 1882, it became The Colored Home and Hospital. In 1899, the institute found a permanent home in the South Bronx, and its mission was slightly altered. "The hospital became a general hospital open to all people without regard to color or creed, although it maintained its founding connection as an institution dedicated to the relief and advancement of the black people. During the hospital's reorganization and eventual occupation of the new site, its name was changed to Lincoln Hospital, to honor the Great Emancipator," President Abraham Lincoln.[116] The philanthropists dedicated more money to the project, ensuring that it would feature some of the latest medical technology and practices. One of the other missions of the institution was that it would educate African Americans how to care for their own health and that of their community.

One of the plans for the newly named Lincoln Hospital and Home was that it would begin training nurses in a formal nursing program. Davis explained:

> Lincoln School for Nurses has a long, proud, and interesting history. This nursing school was one of approximately ten black schools of nursing formed during the 1890s in response to nationwide patterns of racial discrimination and segregation. Lincoln quickly became known as a leader, and it was the only black school of nursing in New York during that era. [117]

Indeed, it was partly the excellent reputation of Lincoln that helped to make Thoms, who would soon graduate from its nursing program, so highly regarded in her field. In 1939, a noted leader in the nursing field said about Lincoln that the school was "not only a leader in the education of colored nurses but one of the leading schools of nursing in the country; and much has been accomplished in the forty-one years of the school's existence. The school has won the respect of the community and has proven that its graduates can hold their own as nurses with the graduates." [118]

The program was strict, giving its female students lessons in nursing as well as in everyday life. Its intent was to prepare them for a career in nursing and to teach them how to be good nurses in all circumstances even those that were not ideal in the least. The nursing students at Lincoln, for example, lived in a dormitory that had only the bare minimum requirements. There was a bed for each student and a small bathroom with two toilets and two bathtubs that 30 women had to share. Not even desks were provided for them to help make their study time more effective—the nurses had to fashion desks from other materials. As Althea T. Davis noted, "This was perhaps their first lesson on improvising—an art required in nursing." [119] The Lincoln Hospital and Home admitted female students between the ages of 21 and 35 years, and these women enrolled in a program whose duration was two years and two months long. This was no small task for many of these young women. Most came from families that were not wealthy and who could have benefited from these women working and earning a paycheck during these 26 months. Davis provided more details about the courses:

> The preliminary course was six months, after which the superintendent of nurses decided whether the student should be retained. If the student were accepted, she had to sign an agreement promising to stay for the remaining two years. The allowance for the first year was $6 and for the second year $7 a month. Each student was given two weeks of vacation a year. Learning continued to be at the bedside and examinations were held frequently. Graduation for each student was contingent upon passing the final examination with a grade of 75 percent or above.[120]

The admissions process was no small task either. The students knew it was an honor to be admitted to the program; they had to take several exams, including exams in English, writing, and oral reading, and they had to bring letters of recommendation from their ministers or doctors, someone who could attest to their spiritual and physical health.[121]

ENTERING THE FIELD

Thoms entered the program in 1903. In 1904, she was offered the position of head nurse on one of the surgical wards. She was selected for this role because of her excellent performance in her courses and her skills at organizing and leadership.[122] These characteristics undoubtedly helped her when she graduated, and she was offered employment at the Lincoln Hospital and Home. In 1905, she was hired as the head nurse for the hospital's operating room, which meant she was a member of the administration, and was assigned responsibility for the entire surgical ward. She must have done her job effectively and successfully; one year later the hospital's administrator's promoted her to the position of assistant superintendent of nurses. During her time at the Lincoln Hospital and Home, Thoms worked diligently to improve and strengthen the curriculum of the nursing program. She kept this position for 18 years until she retired in 1923.

During those 18 years as assistant superintendent of nurses, Thoms's abilities and prowess at organization and management also gained her another role—she served as the acting director of the nursing school from 1906 to 1923. She was never promoted to a full director, and racism was certainly a factor in this decision on the part of the administration to keep Thoms from progressing to a higher level within the hospital. Mabel Staupers, who would eventually become the executive director and later the president of the NACGN, noted years afterward:

> Segregation and discrimination worked against Negroes in another way also. Since the larger schools of nursing were either controlled chiefly by white boards of directors or by white public officials, seldom was a qualified Negro nurse appointed to a high level position. Mrs. Thoms's experience was an example of this type of discrimination. Even though the School of Nursing at Lincoln Hospital was set up as an institution for Negro students, although qualified, Adah Thoms was never appointed as a director. She served in the capacity as director, but was given the title of acting director.[123]

It is quite possible that this experience with racism motivated Adah Belle Samuels Thoms to join forces with Martha Minerva Franklin to promote the establishment of the National Association for Colored Graduate Nurses. Indeed, it is most likely that Thoms wanted to ensure that her own experiences would never be replicated among the next generation of nurses. (For more information on Martha Minerva Franklin, enter her name into any search engine and browse the sites listed.)

MAKING HISTORY

The meeting in New York City, sponsored by the Lincoln Hospital and Home and the Lincoln Nurses Alumnae, has since become a landmark of African-American history, for it was here that the National Association of Colored Graduate Nurses (NACGN) was established. The year, 1908, was also significant. It was the thirtieth anniversary of Mary Eliza Mahoney's graduation from the New England Hospital for Women and Children as America's first trained, African-American nurse.

Many records and biographies of Mahoney state that she cofounded the NACGN. No records, however, specifically indicate that she worked hand-in-hand with Martha Franklin. Instead, Mahoney would meet Franklin a year later and become one of the younger woman's most powerful inspirations.

The three-day meeting in New York was held at St. Mark's Methodist Episcopal Church in August of 1908. Thoms was a member of this church and had secured permission for the meeting to be convened in that location. The meeting opened with a welcome from Thoms, who then introduced Franklin. Franklin addressed the gathering by describing the intent of convening such a meeting. She highlighted the need for improvement in the status and quality of training of African-American nurses. She emphasized that forming a professional association and combining their efforts would lead to a change in the status quo.[124] African-American nurses, she no doubt pointed out, were generally forced to complete their training at segregated schools. After graduation, they took employment offers in which the pay was significantly low and where their nursing duties were often combined with domestic responsibilities, such as cooking, washing, and cleaning. "Franklin convinced the group," wrote Davis, "that this was the only way to stimulate nurses toward a higher standard of nursing, and to raise the requirements for admission to schools of nursing." As Davis also noted, "this national endeavor was welcomed" by the audience of 52 nurses.[125]

THE NACGN'S MISSION

The NACGN's mission was threefold. "The goals of the new organization," according to historical records currently held at the New York Public Library, were "to achieve higher professional standards, to break down discriminatory practices facing black nurses, and to develop leadership among black nurses."[126]

At the NACGN's first meeting, Franklin was elected president and Thoms was elected as the organization's first treasurer.[127] As Franklin had correctly determined, racism and discrimination were preventing African-American nurses from achieving their career goals. Because it served as the major professional association for African-American nurses who were not granted admission to the American Nurses Association (ANA), the NACGN's role became significant.[128]

The NACGN had a difficult beginning, however, since membership rates remained surprisingly low. The reason for this is unclear, but one possibility is that communication was not as widespread and effective as it could have been, given the geographic distribution of NACGN members. In the first few years, therefore, the organization's greatest task was to compile a registry of African-American nurses working across the country.[129]

BEGINNING CHALLENGES

The NACGN's membership rates were so low in the beginning that only 26 nurses attended the organization's first national convention, which was held in Boston in 1909. This convention marked the first time that either Franklin or Thoms had met the legendary Mahoney, but it was the beginning of a friendship and comradeship that would become a powerful force in molding opportunities for African Americans in nursing. Mahoney addressed the convention attendees, and her words inspired everyone with a sense of hopefulness for the future. According to Thoms, Mahoney, in her welcoming address to the 26 members present in Boston, had remarked that "one of the problems which had always distressed her was the condition in the early days of her training, when colored girls who applied for admission to good schools usually found the doors closed against them, though she said my school [the Lincoln Hospital and Home] was not so selfish, she knew other schools of nursing were."[130] Although she was perturbed by the apparent decline in quality of training of African-American nurses in comparison to her own training, Mahoney must have been pleased by the progress made so far. Since she had graduated 30 years earlier as the first trained African-American nurse, thousands had followed her into the profession. Indeed, because of her early support for and affiliation with the NACGN, Mahoney quickly emerged as an ideal emblem of the aspirations and potential achievements of African-American nurses.

Franklin and Thoms used the first convention—which was also the NACGN's second meeting—to start strengthening the organization. Franklin worked on establishing state-level associations of African-American nurses, which would function as local chapters of the national-level NACGN. Franklin chose the 10 states in which these chapters would be established and then appointed 10 nurses to serve as chairpersons of these local chapters.[131]

DISCRIMINATION IN THE FIELD

The NACGN faced many obstacles, especially segregation, which had become a sad reality for those working in the professions. In 1896, the Supreme Court's decision in the case of *Plessy* v. *Ferguson* had established the "separate but equal" rule for American educational institutions, denying African Americans admission to predominantly white schools on the presumption that a parallel entity existed for African Americans. Schools became more officially divided into white-only or black-only, a condition that had long been the norm in the United States but which *Plessy* v. *Ferguson* formalized.

Mahoney had graduated from the New England Hospital for Women and Children in 1879, and it has been widely acknowledged as a testimonial to her excellent performance that the school continued to admit African-American women to the program. Seventeen years after her graduation, however, she saw a law enacted that essentially prevented her African-American colleagues from studying and benefiting from an education at the nation's top schools. It is not surprising that she placed her support behind the NACGN, intent on making a change in the alarming atmosphere of segregation and mounting racism.

By the time of Mahoney's death, approximately 2,500 African-American women were graduate nurses who had completed professional training programs—mostly from one of the many black-only nursing schools across the country. About two-thirds of them worked as private nurses or in institutions, such as hospitals or homes for the elderly or infirm.[132] There existed a wide chasm of hostility between white nurses and African-American nurses during this time, the mid-1920s, mostly because African-American nurses made less money. In Virginia, the State Board of Health employed 36 white nurses, each of whom earned $125 per month, and one African-American nurse, who earned only $100 per month. Their duties, needless to say, were parallel in difficulty and dedication.[133] In other parts of Virginia, some white nurses made $110 a month while their African-American counterparts made $80. The wage difference in other southern states, like Alabama and Tennessee, was even more staggering. White nurses earned $110 and African-American nurses earned $65.[134]

Racism in the nursing field was quite blatant. In Chicago, the chief nurse of the City Health Department, Margaret Butler, was recorded as saying that white nurses were preferable to African-American nurses because the skills of the latter group were "inferior to that of the white nurses, they are not punctual, and are incapable of analyzing a social situation."[135] Darlene Clark Hine further summarized the remarks made by this Chicago nursing leader:

> Butler added that, in her opinion, black nurses did poor clerical work and were able to be used only among the black population. Moreover, she declared that even 'the colored group,' if presented a choice, preferred the services of a white nurse. Without elaborating on the specifics of the racial friction between black and white nurses, Butler asserted that black nurses created problems because of their marked tendency 'to organize against authority' and 'to engage in political intrigue.'[136]

The last comment made by Butler, on the tendency of African-American nurses to organize against the white authorities of their work environments, clearly indicates that African-American nurses felt their jobs were under threat and that they organized to protect themselves. Similar comments by white nursing authorities were made during this time period. Another prominent Chicago leader said she resented the organizing abilities of African-American nurses because it meant that she could not fire an African-American nurse without "stirring up trouble."[137]

LIMITATIONS
The blatant racism that permeated the field of nursing meant that opportunities for African-American nurses were limited. According to Darlene Clark Hine:

African-American students. Although this did not produce concrete results, the NACGN persevered. In 1916, the organization joined forces with the National Association for the Advancement of Colored People (NAACP) to improve the quality of existing African-American schools. The method they settled upon was to raise admissions standards. This would result in a higher quality level of nursing graduates as well as more respect for the schools themselves. Adah Belle Samuels Thoms was especially insistent that these schools require a high school diploma as a prerequisite for all applicants. The road to progress was quite slow, but improvement was on the horizon.

ORGANIZING

The National Association of Colored Graduate Nurses, under the leadership of Franklin and Thoms, continued to hold meetings of African-American nurses on a regular basis. Whenever she could, Mary Eliza Mahoney attended these meetings, contributing much to the positive, energetic atmosphere.

The spirits of the nurses and the officials of the NACGN were already high at these meetings. Progress was slowly being made. The NACGN was being recognized by others in the nursing profession as the main voice of African-American nurses. Regular meetings helped African-American nurses network with one another and get updates on the status of the profession. The meetings also helped clarify the difficulties that they still collectively faced.

In early 1916, Adah Belle Samuels Thoms was elected president of the NACGN. Like Franklin, she focused on increasing the membership of the organization. Soon after assuming her new role in the organization, she embarked on an arduous traveling schedule. She visited African-American nurses all over the country, speaking about the mission of the NACGN and encouraging those she met to join the organization and establish new local chapters. In April of 1916, for example, she traveled to Virginia and met with the Norfolk Nurses Association. Soon after the meeting, the members of that association organized and formed a large and active chapter of the National Association of Colored Graduate Nurses.[143] It is certainly due to her charisma and her ability to translate to others the urgent need to organize and work together to improve the status of African-American nurses that the NACGN's membership increased steadily.

6　Battling for
Acceptance

VOICING THE CHALLENGES

The ninth convention of the NACGN was held in New York City in August of 1916. At this convention, Adah Belle Samuels Thoms composed a song and presented it to the members:

> In this warfare we have listed
> Sisters, one and all;
> Let us always be united,
> Waiting for the call.
> Ever seeking to relieve thee,
> Onward thus we go;
> By His aid we will restore thee,
> Trusting ever more.
> Never doubting never fearing,
> Ours the onward march;
> Ask His guidance, always trusting
> Jesus, all in all.
> We with gentle hands care thee
> Happy to be near thee,
> Never doubting, always trusting,
> Trusting God, our all.[144]

This song by Thoms was representative of the religious faith to which she—and many of the NACGN members—adhered. Many African-American nurses viewed their religious faith as one of the chief motivations for entering a profession dedicated to caring for others and nursing their fellow humans back to health. In fact, Thoms's song was adopted by the membership as the official anthem of the National Association of Colored Graduate Nurses.

At this convention, Thoms delivered her first address as president to the general membership. Her words, reprinted below, stirred the NACGN's members and cemented Thoms's role as an inspirational leader. In the speech, Thoms explained some of the most pressing challenges that she and her colleagues faced. The address also helps to illustrate Thoms's personality and her optimistic attitude about the mission of the NACGN:

> Sister Nurses, Ladies and Gentlemen: It is my pleasure to greet you at this, our Ninth Annual Convention, to present to you some of our problems of the past year, which has indeed been one of great moment, and very eventful to the nursing world at large. We have faced difficulties of various kinds, those that have confronted us most gravely, being State Registration and Post-Graduate Work in some of the larger training schools, the latter being so necessary to those of us that have graduated from small schools. While they have offered the best at hand, our nurses feel that in order to meet the present day demands and keep abreast of the times, they must seek to admittance to some of the larger schools offering a Post-Graduate Course, or if there be no such course offered, make appeals to the governing board asking that such a course be established in these respective schools. Now that training schools are being conducted in a manner that calls for the most favorable references and the highest standards of efficiency for the pupil, the States, likewise, demanding registration of its graduates; I fail to see why there should be any question about any qualified nurse sitting in examination with her more fortunate sisters, just as her physicians and surgeons. Is it not a fact that the two professions go hand in hand? It is not a small thing to be admitted into the homes of rich and poor alike, to be left in charge by day and by night with some loved one of that home, with an occasional visit from the family physician who depends entirely upon the watchfulness of the nurse, and accuracy of her reports for the safe restoration to health of that dear one, and yet feel that

there is a law, or an examining board in any State, controlled perhaps partly by the same physician who knows the value of that nurse if no other. Must we feel that he would sit idly by and permit that board, without raising a dissenting voice, to abrogate so valuable an assistant? I feel that the time has come when we as graduate nurses of Standardized Training Schools should take up this matter very seriously and seek an interview with the Board of Nurse Examiners in every state in the Union where registration is required, for it is my unbiased conviction that nursing is the broadest professional field open to women today. Therefore I urge you to prepare yourselves to meet the present day needs and future demands. While we have faced these problems, they have been equally balanced with brighter outlooks for our future. We may congratulate ourselves upon the work that we are doing along special lines, yet I do not feel that we should be satisfied until we have placed our National Association on a much stronger basis and raised its tower so high that it will stand out like a beacon light. The field for nurses today is very wide; it is no longer confined to the sickroom. It covers the nurseries, the milk stations, the schools, the playgrounds, factories, stores, the districts, the courts; social service and various avenues now open to the graduate nurse. And by united effort of the members of this association, more of us shall engage in these activities. We as nurses should stand very close together, closer than any other women in public life; we should have deeper sympathies, more interests in common. For no other women pass through the same discouraging period of loneliness and criticism of uphill struggles and ingratitude as the nurses; not only through her training, but in after life. It has been my pleasure during the past year to search for those that were apparently lost from our ranks. Of the 742 letters sent out by your presiding officer, 512 replies have been received from my coworkers, each one expressing her faith and loyalty and pledging her support towards standardizing the profession of nursing along social, moral, economic, and Christian lines. I also visited many of the homes of our members; wherever I went, the welcome was most cordial, each one seemed interested and doing a splendid work, not only happy to be one of us but eager too, that others should be. Each time I returned home stimulated and encouraged, feeling that my efforts were not in vain.... It may also interest you to know, that of the 100,000 nurses of which this country is proud today; that we number about 920. I further welcome this opportunity to express my sincere thanks to the officers and members of this Association for their loyal support during the year, and deeply appreciate the honor bestowed upon me at our last meeting to serve you in this capacity. If in the slightest degree I have met your approval, permit me to say, it is due entirely to your excellent and hearty co-operation, for which I offer my heart-felt thanks. And this thought I leave with you: If we wish to succeed in this great work that we have undertaken, we must be earnest, we must be courageous, we must be imbued with absolute determination. Remember that every door of opportunity is open to women, and the professional nurse may find therein a place for herself. Let unity and service be our watchword, and may this Association always stand for this highest standard of nursing, and for the purest ideals of true womanhood.[145]

The most prominent themes in her speech emphasized constant progress through unity and individual hard work. Thoms focused on progress for women as well as progress for those in the nursing profession; this feminism was one of the cornerstones of her advocacy of the NACGN's mission.

WORLD WAR I

The Civil War and the Spanish-American War had given African-American nurses a chance to prove that they could effectively and competently serve their nation. World War I, the "war to end all wars," also showed African-American nurses how tragic their circumstances could be.

World War I began in 1914, but the United States did not enter the conflict until three years later. The war was the deadliest in history (at least, until World War II), resulting in the deaths of 10 million. Ending an era when wars were fought by soldiers on defined battlefields, World War I was fought in an unprecedented way. Bombs fell from the sky on soldiers and civilians alike while soldiers crawled into trenches and fired on the enemy. As in all wars, people suffered from infection and starvation. Many of the soldiers who survived the war returned to their homes with injuries that prevented them from resuming normal lives. Their injuries were mental as well as physical. According to William Keylor, "Others suffered the lasting effects of what in those days was called shell shock and what is today labeled post-traumatic stress disorder, a psychological affliction that prevents a successful adaptation to civilian life." [146]

DISCRIMINATION IN BATTLE

The Red Cross, which oversaw the Armed Forces Nurse Corps, issued a call for nurses to enlist and volunteer to serve in the war. The American Nurses Association (ANA), which had denied admission to African-American nurses, was one of the organizations that responded to the call, encouraging nurses to sign up to serve. As usual, nurses considered it an honor to volunteer and serve their nation by helping care for the wounded and the ill.

African-American nurses inquired about whether their applications to enlist would be considered. They were informed by the head of the Red Cross that "we are enrolling colored nurses at the present time and shall continue to do so in order that they may be available if at any time there is an opportunity to assign them to duty in military hospitals."[147] In 1916, Adah Belle Samuels Thoms informed the NACGN membership that many African-American nurses had demonstrated an interest in enlisting:

> On June 29th the managers of Lincoln Hospital offered to equip a "Base Hospital Unit" and give colored registered nurses an opportunity to become members of the Red Cross Corps. This offer was accepted at Washington at a cost of $25,000,000 with an enrollment of 65 nurses. I am pleased to inform you that within 28 hours 31 of this number had offered their names in answer to the appeal and at the present time there are 87 of these noble women ready to enroll for duty at the front if called. This proved loyalty, in loyalty there is unity, in unity there must be strength.[148]

It was important to Thoms and the NACGN leadership that African-American nurses be permitted to serve during World War I. Althea T. Davis speculated on the reasons for this:

> Soldiers who had sustained injuries were ill, and race did not make a different to those in pain, trying to repair an injury, or convalesce. . . . They [Thoms and the NACGN] believed it was an opportunity to serve their country, change their low status, demonstrate their abilities, and for White American nurses to develop a trust in this group of nurses as colleagues and competent practitioners. . . . Even though this group of Black nurses knew they were considered second-class citizens,

they felt this was still their country and they would like to come together with White Americans in time of war.[149]

In other words, by serving in the war beside white nurses, African-American nurses would signal that they were their equals and their colleagues and that nationality was more important than race.

FALSE IMPLICATIONS

Even though many African-American nurses volunteered, few were recruited to serve as part of the Armed Forces Nurse Corps. One year after Thoms delivered her hopeful assessment of the possibility of the military's enrollment of African-American nurses, none had been called to duty. Despite inquiries, no satisfactory answers or explanations for this were given.[150] Even though the majority of the African-American nurses who volunteered for service met the required standards for enlistment, the impression that they lacked the required training to serve prevailed. To some extent, the basis for this reasoning was grounded in a half-truth—the only training available to African-American nurses was at the poorly funded black hospitals and nursing schools around the country. The fact that these institutions provided high quality education was simply ignored.

Thoms was especially incensed by this treatment of African-American nurses, possibly because the crisis caused by the war had prompted the Lincoln Hospital and Home to temporarily place her in the position of superintendent. While she was making major administrative decisions at one of the most prominent African-American hospitals in the nation, she was receiving none of the credit. Furthermore, she was unable to exert any influence on behalf of her African-American colleagues.

1917 NACGN CONVENTION

At the NACGN convention in 1917, one year after she had delivered her hopeful words about the high enlistment numbers of African-American nurses into the military, Thoms gave a presidential address that was far different in tone:

> I feel as if we are in the midst of a great political campaign. It is true the government has not yet found it convenient to accept us in the American Red Cross Nursing Association as the individual or in the group, yet I know that this body of well trained women is ready to stand as a unit in answer to the nation's call to contribute this 'bit' towards alleviating the suffering of humanity. Let us keep within us the spirit of preparedness—nursing preparedness which means nothing more than doing our full duty along the lines assigned to us in church, society, and state—being ready to meet every emergency and give the very best that within us lies. It is a fact that we cannot at this time serve at the front with our more fortunate sisters by profession. Perhaps there remains for us a greater work at home. The spirit we show, the methods we adopt and results accomplished will best determine our future throughout the world with all races. It is for us to outline our course. Let us find our place in our own way, along some special line, then hold to our purpose. If we cannot serve in a base hospital or be nurses on the battlefield, the service we render in our own communities will count for just as much, if wisely directed.[151]

CHANGES

African-American nurses found themselves deeply disappointed in the American government and military during the period of World War I. Rather than focus on their frustration with segregation, however, they determined not to allow themselves and their profession to be disregarded in such a manner again. A series of events that took places in after World War I led to a slow change in the attitude towards nursing and African-American professionals in the field.

In the late 1920s and 1930s, the conditions in American hospitals vastly improved; they were no longer places where only the poor and lower class went to spend their last days. Gone were the days when hospitals crawled with vermin and germs and people had a greater chance of dying than of surviving. As hospitals began to improve, they admitted patients from the middle classes, and the demand for private nurses dwindled.[152]

The job market for nurses in hospitals and institutions was flooded with out-of-work nurses, many of whom were African American. As nurses of both races were hired by hospitals, African-American and white nurses began to work side-by-side. White nurses generally resented their African-American colleagues. They felt that their jobs were threatened because African-Americans nurses would often agree to work for lower wages. Their resentment also reflected a snobbish attitude. According to Hine, "Among practically all groups of white nurses, whether involved in hospital work, private practice, educational institutions, public-health associations, or professional organizations, located in the North or South, the predominant image of the black nurse was that of a professional, moral, and social inferior." [153]

During this transitional period, African-American nurses continued to be denied admission to the American Red Cross, the American Nursing Association, and the Armed Forces Nurses Corps. Despite these obstacles, organizations like the National Association of Colored Graduate Nurses continued to work diligently to gain acceptance for their members.

ESTELLE MASSEY RIDDLE OSBORNE

Things continued to change slowly. In 1931, Estelle Massey Riddle Osborne became the first African-American woman to earn a master's degree in nursing. Three years later, the NACGN elected her as its president. She, in turn, hired Mabel

K. Staupers as the first executive director of the organization in 1934. There was no better duo for the job of resuscitating the NACGN. Their energy, charisma, and intelligence marked one of the most productive periods in the history of the NACGN.

Born in Texas in1903, Riddle received her nursing degree from the Homer G. Phillips Hospital in St. Louis, Missouri. She passed the Missouri State Board Examination with an extraordinarily high score of 93.3 percent.[154] After her graduation, she worked at the Homer G. Phillips Hospital and was eventually given an appointment that promoted her to an administrative position. Since all African-American nurses had previously worked under white administrators, this was a major achievement. Riddle was the first African-American person to overcome that obstacle in the profession of nursing.

In 1927, Riddle moved to New York City and enrolled at Columbia University. She earned a bachelor's degree in nursing education three years later; the following year, she earned a master's degree. In doing so, she became the first African-American woman to complete a master's degree in nursing education.[155]

The nursing school at Harlem Hospital recruited Riddle as a part-time instructor, and she also became an active member of the National Council of Negro Women (NCNW). She eventually left New York City for Washington, D.C., where Freedmen's Hospital appointed her its educational director.[156] Within only a few years of completing her degree, Riddle had catapulted into the role of one of the most prominent African-American nurses and nursing scholars in the nation.

MABEL STAUPERS

Riddle's partner in the cause of championing the rights of African-American nurses was Mabel Staupers. Staupers's credentials, even before she met Riddle and became involved in the NACGN, were quite impressive, and Riddle energetically recruited her to the cause.

Mabel Staupers was born Mabel Doyle in Barbados, West Indies, in 1890. She emigrated from the West Indies to New York in 1903 when she was only 13 years old. In 1917, at the age of 27, she married James Max Keaton. That same year she received her nursing degree from Freedmen's Hospital School of Nursing (now Howard University College of Nursing) in Washington, D.C.

In 1920, Staupers moved back to New York where she joined forces with Louis T. Wright and James Wilson. Wright and Wilson were African-American physicians whose goal was to establish a hospital with African-American staff that would treat African-American patients. Through the combined efforts of Staupers, Wright, and Wilson, the dream was realized and became the Booker T. Washington Sanitarium. Staupers was appointed director of nurses. The experiment was successful, and Staupers's role in organizing the effort made her well known and respected.

Staupers eventually moved to Philadelphia when the Mudget Hospital offered her a position as superintendent of nurses. She accepted the offer because she knew that the key to advancing herself as an African-American nurse was to gain more experience in health administration.

Staupers also became involved in fighting against discrimination in educational institutions. As Estelle Riddle noted, few African-American nurses were able to obtain supervisory and administrative positions. It was typical to find a hospital staff composed exclusively of African Americans headed by a white administrator. Riddle estimated that "One-third of the schools for Negro nurses [were] supervised by white superintendents and administrators."[157] The only way for African-American women to advance into these higher-status and higher-paying positions was through better education and advanced nursing degrees. The diplomas most African-American training schools issued were not on a par with bachelor's and master's degrees awarded by other institutions.

Staupers understood that the only way to further her own career and to open doors for other African-American women in the profession would be to break down the obstacles keeping them from advancing to higher positions in the field. Like Riddle, she knew that the credentials of African-American nurses were always called into question even though they had finished nursing programs similar to those white nurses had completed. To this end, while in Philadelphia, she worked with the members of the Pennsylvania state board on ways to stan- dardize training for all nurses.[158] She also completed a fellowship at the Henry Phipps Institute for Tuberculosis in Philadelphia.

Staupers also worked on producing research on the health needs of African Americans. Back in New York, she began to conduct surveys on the health needs of Harlem's residents.[159] The health status of the African-American community was not receiv- ing much attention from other medical professionals, illustrating another of racism's effects. According to Darlene Clark Hine, the survey on Harlem's residents proved to be a significant one:

> The report evaluated the services available to blacks in the city and state tuberculosis facilities. Her work on the pro- ject attracted attention and acclaim. The survey became the rationale for the establishment of the Harlem Committee of the New York Tuberculosis and Health Association. She was appointed the association's first executive secretary, a position which enabled her to meet and form close friend- ships with black political and social elites in the city. For the next twelve years Staupers served in this position.[160]

While her professional stature grew during this time, Staupers's marriage was suffering. She and her husband, James Max Keaton, divorced for reasons that are unclear. She eventually married again, this time to Fritz C. Staupers, in 1931. Her second husband died in 1949, leaving her a young widow.[161] Staupers never had children.

By the time she was recruited by Riddle, Staupers was in her 40s and had experienced severe discrimination on a professional level. It was these experiences that helped turn Staupers into an advocate for all African-American nurses. As Sylvia Coleman wrote in an article on trailblazers in nursing, "After graduating with honors from Freedmen's Hospital School of Nursing in Washington, D.C., Staupers challenged opposition she encountered from segregated nursing organizations. Her campaign was not a self-centered climb up the nursing ladder, but rather a determination to expand health care options for African Americans by stamping out segregation."[162]

SIGNS OF HOPE

Riddle and Staupers made a dynamic team in confronting overt discrimination in the field of African-American nursing. They dedicated themselves to tearing down the barriers of segregation. According to Darlene Clark Hine, "The emergence of two talented black nursing leaders, Estelle Massey Riddle and Mabel K. Staupers, who eagerly assumed the reins of the fledgling NACGN and worked assiduously to resuscitate it, proved most critical to the mobilization of the entire black nursing organization."[163]

Staupers researched some of the specific barriers preventing the progress of African-American nurses, including the reasons why many nursing schools had closed their doors to them. According to Althea T. Davis, "Staupers analyzed that white nursing administrators thought that black nursing students could only adequately care for black patients, and that they were in fact happier and/or more comfortable in black schools of nursing. This rationalization was indeed self-serving and aimed at preserving segregation as the status quo."[164]

CHALLENGING THE DOUBLE STANDARD

The primary goal was to convince the American Nursing Association to admit African-American nurses. To be admitted to the ANA, all nurses had to be members of the State Nurses Association in their respective states. It was these state associations that—in 16 different states as well as Washington D.C.—barred African-American nurses from membership. Riddle and Staupers traveled across the nation, bringing the issue of segregation in the nursing profession to the attention of anyone who could make a difference. "For 12 consecutive years, Riddle and Staupers attended each ANA House of Delegates meeting, lobbying for complete integration of Black nurses into their professional association." [165]

Their efforts generated much discussion and controversy. They asserted the position of the NACGN that "the entire profession of nursing could not progress as long as any one group of nurses was required to face a double standard....

American Nurses Association

For years, the leaders and members of the NACGN sought membership and inclusion in the American Nurses Association (ANA), the premier professional organization of American nurses.

The ANA was founded in 1896 in New York City by five nurses, who chose to name their organization the Nurses' Associated Alumnae of the United States and Canada. Their intent was to restore the solid reputation of nursing, which had become corrupted as a result of unqualified people working privately and in hospitals as nurses. At the group's first meeting in 1897 in Baltimore, Maryland, they outlined their goals: "To establish and maintain a code of ethics; to elevate the standard of nursing education; to promote the usefulness and honor, the financial and other interests of nursing."*

In 1911, the group changed its name to the American Nurses Association. The ANA grew rapidly. In 1912, it convened and discussed the need for more nurses in the field of public health. This led to the establishment of the National Organization of Public Health Nursing (NOPHN), an effort to

Black nurses desired no special privileges or waivers and made their position known to the members of the various state boards of nurse examiners through the NACGN."[166] It would be a long time, however, before Riddle and Staupers would see their efforts come to fruition.

1934 REGIONAL CONFERENCE

In 1934, in response to the challenges faced by African-American nurses, the NACGN organized its first regional conference at Lincoln Hospital and Home in New York, the same site where the organization had held its inaugural meeting. The conference was attended by officials of the National Medical Association, the National Organization for Public Health Nursing, and the National Health Circle for

make the public aware of preventive health practices. The establishment of the NOPHN also helped to clarify the diversity developing within the field of nursing. In 1913, the ANA joined the American Red Cross and began to minister to rural communities as well as urban communities.**

World Wars I and II created an urgent need for nurses in the military. In the 1940s, the ANA encouraged the creation of the U.S. Nurse Cadet Corps, a program in which the United States government would subsidize the education of nursing students in exchange for their military service.***

Today, the ANA continues to lead the nursing profession in responding to medical crises, advocating fair health care access, and maintaining the profession's high standards.

* "Voices from the Past, Visions of the Future," *http://www.nursingworld.org/centenn/index.htm* (Retrieved February 18, 2004).

** Ibid.

*** Ibid.

Colored People, among others. The agenda of the conference had a specific focus. Specific issues to be addressed were

> ... the impact of the economic crisis on the salaries and wages of black nurses; the urgent need to train more black public-health nurses; the continued discrimination against and denial of admission of black nurses to universities offering advanced courses in nursing; the difficulty inherent in improving the black hospital nursing schools; and finally the need to develop the NACGN.[167]

The idea was to make the NACGN the main channel for African-American nurses to help them attain their goals and stay current with nursing trends and techniques. Another focal point of the conference was to design ways to help white nurses and nursing leaders understand the dilemma of their African-American counterparts. As Hine noted, "Try as they might to avoid the issue, some white nurse leaders were well aware that the day was near when they would have to confront and revoke policies contributing to the professional ostracism of the black nurse."[168] The NACGN was determined to play a role in hastening this process.

BENEFACTORS

Shortly after the regional conference, which was considered a significant revival of the NACGN, the association benefited from two significant contributors: Frances Payne Bolton and the Julius Rosenwald Fund.

Bolton was a wealthy heiress from Cleveland, Ohio, who had taken an interest in the nursing profession. Although there is no indication that she ever pursued it as a career for herself, she served on the advisory council of the National Organization for Public Health Nursing and was also director of the Cleveland Visiting Nurses Association. Her husband, Chester Bolton, was a U.S. Congressman; when he died suddenly in

1939, she served out his term in the House of Representatives. During this period, she designed the 1943 Bolton Bill, which created a U.S. Cadet Nurses program.[169]

Although Bolton certainly used her influence and her wealth to advance the profession of nursing, her interest in the NACGN in the early 1930s is unclear. According to Hine, "Although she was a long-time friend of nurses and a strong advocate of their interests, it is not altogether clear why she desired to assist in the transformation of the NACGN into a potent weapon with which black nurses could mount a sustained attack against the exclusion and discriminatory treatment they suffered."[170] Bolton gave the NACGN $250 in 1934 but soon increased her donation. Until 1951, she gave $2,000 a year to the organization. Most historians agree that the amount of money she donated, and which the NACGN could depend upon in its budget, paid a great part of the association's annual operating expenses. The NACGN wanted to do something to acknowledge her generosity, but Bolton preferred to remain in the background regarding all her charitable work.

Also in 1934, the Julius Rosenwald Fund donated $1,250 to the organization and continued its sponsorship annually. The funds were made possible through the advocacy of M.O. Bousfield, an African-American doctor who was an associate director of the fund's division on African-American health issues. Bousfield was a colleague of several of the leaders of the NACGN. With these new, generous funds, the NACGN was able to hire a full-time executive director and rent space for its headquarters at the Rockefeller Center where other nursing organizations also had their headquarters. The funds also paid many of the travel expenses of the NACGN leadership who could now travel to various regions of the country to spread the mission of the organization and its ideals.[171]

7 Integration at Last

WORLD WAR II

In her book, *Black Women in White: Racial Conflict and Cooperation in the Nursing Profession, 1890–1950,* Darlene Clark Hine wrote:

> It is a supreme irony that nursing's fortune is so often connected to war. Florence Nightingale's experiences in the Crimean War, the appalling casualties of the American Civil War, and the death and destruction of World War I all influenced the emergence and development of nursing training and practice. In the wake of these shocking episodes of massive carnage, nursing reaped increased status and greater public esteem.[172]

When World War II began, leaders from nursing associations and organizations around the country met to discuss ways in which they could best mobilize their nurses to serve the nation and aid the war effort. What resulted was a new, national entity called the National Nursing Council for War Service. The National Association of Colored Graduate Nurses was represented on the council by leaders such as Mabel Staupers who was intent on making sure that the error of World War I—when African-American nurses enlisted but were not asked to serve—would not be repeated. "I have every belief," she said, "that since we were voluntarily requested to become part of the Nursing Council on National Defense and since the national survey of nurses is being sent to Negro nurses, we will not be left out."[173]

INCREASING THE PRESSURE

As America's involvement in the war became clear, Staupers increased the pressure on the government and the War Department to include African-American nurses and allow them to serve in the military effort. She formed a National Defense Committee of the NACGN, and she appointed highly regarded and well-respected African-American nurses from across the United States to serve as members.

In 1940, she arranged for a meeting with the members of the NACGN National Defense Committee and herself with the Surgeon General of the United States Army, James C. Magee. The reason for the meeting with Magee was Magee's own announcement that no African Americans or other persons of color would serve in the military until the military hospitals could designate separate "colored wards" in accordance with segregationist practices in parts of the United States at the time. Staupers, of course, feared that this was just another tactic to prevent African-American nurses from serving. Perhaps Magee's comment that his plan was "segregation without discrimination" served to further aggravate the situation, especially since it was obvious that segregation itself was inherently discriminatory.[174]

The NACGN and others in the African-American community harshly criticized the military's position on this matter, but the military resisted change, insisting that "the Medical Department has not discriminated in any sense against the Negro medical profession, nurses, or enlisted men."[175] Military authorities believed that, by providing separate facilities, they were offering African Americans a grand opportunity to serve; they did not admit that the actual separation itself was an act of racial discrimination. Nonetheless, by allowing African-American nurses to serve only in segregated wards, and by making the existence of those wards contingent upon sufficient quotas of African-American soldiers, the military was preventing many willing African-American nurses from serving their country. It was also ensuring that white American soldiers would not be nursed back to health by African Americans. Magee himself commented on this point: "It is not intended that colored nurses or colored physicians be engaged in the care and treatment of military personnel other than colored."[176] This policy implied that the quality of education and experience of African-American nurses was somehow lacking. It was also blatantly racist.

The attempt by the military to sugarcoat the issue would not work with the NACGN. As Staupers said, "My position is that, as long as either one of the Services reject Negro nurses, they are discriminated against and as long as either Service continues to assign them to duty as separated units, they are segregated." [177] She also said, "We fail to understand how America can say to the world that in this country we are ready to defend democracy when the world that in this country we are ready to defend democracy when its Army and Navy are committed to a policy of discrimination." [178]

During the meeting between Magee and the NACGN National Defense Committee, it was proposed that there be a quota established for African-American nurses to serve in the military. Staupers was not happy with this suggestion, but she did have the foresight to see that a quota was at least a sign of progress; further progress—such as the lifting of quotas and the service of nurses based on qualifications only—could come later. She accepted the proposal temporarily.

Nevertheless, Staupers immediately organized protests against the quota system she had agreed to. She also sought the help of white American nurses, hoping to present a united front of nurses against the military's discriminatory policy. According to Hine, "Staupers' determination to fight the War Department quotas using every means at her disposal grew out of an awareness that the American public's appreciation for nurses and the status of the nursing profession improved markedly whenever the country was involved in a war." [179] She knew that if America saw African-American women bravely caring for wounded and ill soldiers in the midst of battle, the cause would gain support.

Slowly the battle began to be won. The African-American nurses who enlisted under the quota system served well and effectively. In April 1941, the Army Nurse Corps admitted 56

African-American nurses; in July 1942, it admitted another 60. These nurses, however, were assigned only to hospitals that treated soldiers of color and German prisoners of war.[180] Staupers continued her pressure tactics, continuing to organize protests and write letters to the Army and Navy.

ENTER MRS. ROOSEVELT

The resistance of the military to having African-American nurses care for white American soldiers finally led Staupers to take even more drastic measures. She arranged a meeting between herself and First Lady Eleanor Roosevelt who was known as a social progressive and an open-minded woman. Eleanor Roosevelt agreed to the meeting, which took place in

Eleanor Roosevelt

Anna Eleanor Roosevelt is remembered in history as a social reformer and a champion of America's underprivileged communities. She created a legend for herself as a voice for the voiceless.

She was born in 1884 to Anna Hall and Elliott Roosevelt, both of whom passed away by the time she was 10 years old. Before she was 20, she had met and become engaged to Franklin Delano Roosevelt, a distant relative of her father's. The Roosevelts were a prominent family, especially President Theodore Roosevelt, the elder brother of Eleanor's father Elliott. In 1905, Eleanor and Franklin married, and over the next several years, Eleanor gave birth to six children.*

Franklin Delano Roosevelt set his sights on the White House. With Eleanor at his side, he embarked on a long and successful political career, beginning with the Senate where he served from 1910 to 1913. He held a number of other political offices, and it became known in Washington that the intelligent and keen Eleanor served as his advisor and

November 1944. There is some indication that Staupers had hinted before the meeting that she would spread the word about the discriminatory policies affecting African-American nurses. Because 1944 was an election year, publicizing the issue might affect Franklin Delano Roosevelt's chances of reelection. Whatever the case, Eleanor Roosevelt was convinced that a meeting with Staupers was a necessity, as was solving the issue of discrimination in the military.

Staupers described to the First Lady the hypocrisy within the military and the discrimination that prevented African-American nurses to tend to white American soldiers. She also emphasized the negative implications that arose from assigning African-American nurses to care for German prisoners

confidante in personal as well as political matters. When her husband was diagnosed with polio in 1921, a disease which left him in a wheelchair, she helped him regain his strength and focus on his goals.**

In 1933, FDR assumed the office of the presidency, and Eleanor set about reforming the traditional role of First Lady. Although she still carried out the traditional social obligations of entertaining that came with the job, she also tackled more serious issues. She visited slums, set up schools in poor areas, worked for the Red Cross, and advocated equal rights. She worked tirelessly with the United Nations, helping to found UNICEF and chairing the UN Human Rights Commission. After the death of FDR in 1945, she continued to campaign for human rights until her own death in 1962.

* Anna Eleanor Roosevelt,"
  http://www.whitehouse.gov/history/firstladies/ar32.html
** Ibid.

of war: "When our women hear of the great need for nurses in the Army and when they enter the service it is with the high hopes that they will be used to nurse sick and wounded soldiers who are fighting our country's enemies and not primarily to care for these enemies."[181]

As a result of this meeting, Eleanor Roosevelt contacted the new Surgeon General of the United States Army, Norman T. Kirk, who had succeeded Magee in 1943. Kirk, however, adhered to the policy of his predecessor and confirmed that it was unthinkable to allow African-American nurses to care for white American soldiers. He did not change his views until 1945 when a shortage of nurses in the military suddenly changed the circumstances.

At a meeting Kirk convened in 1945 in New York City, he announced that the military was considering instituting a draft to recruit more nurses into active service. Staupers, not surprisingly, attended this meeting. She stood up and addressed Kirk directly before the audience that had gathered: "If nurses are needed so desperately, why isn't the Army using colored nurses? ... Of 9,000 registered Negro nurses the Army has taken 247, the Navy takes none."[182] The Surgeon General challenged her numbers, but she stood firm and demanded an answer. According to Darlene Clark Hine, "News of the Staupers-Kirk exchange received nationwide coverage and made the headlines of virtually every black newspaper in the country."[183]

More importantly, the heated debate brought the issue of racial discrimination in the military to the forefront of national issues. "Why," people asked themselves, "shouldn't African-American nurses serve their country? Why should race be an obstacle when people's lives and national security are at stake?"

A massive public outcry against the idea of drafting white American nurses while ignoring thousands of willing African-American nurses was soon directed at the White House. The leaders of the NACGN stated publicly that the military must lift the use of quotas and segregated military hospital and admit nurses regardless of their race. Such an act "would demonstrate to young Negro women who are considering nursing as a career the fact that opportunities to serve will not be denied them, thus paving the way for a greater contribution by Negroes after the war to the health not only of Negroes but of the whole population."[184] Staupers called on nursing organizations and African-American advocacy groups across the country to stand up in support of the NACGN's efforts to encourage the military to integrate. Her efforts finally met with success.

In January 1945, the United States military declared that the system of using quotas was finally over. First, the Army said it would admit nurses without consideration of their race. The Navy also finally caved in on this point and admitted African-American nurses. A few weeks later, Phyllis Daley, an African-American nurse, was inducted into the Navy Nurse Corps. Staupers and the National Association of Colored Graduate Nurses had triumphed over racial discrimination and had won new recognition and respect for African-American nurses.

THE FINAL FRONTIER

There was one battle left to be won: African-American nurses had still not been allowed admittance into the American Nurses Association (ANA), which was the major professional organization in the field. Staupers and Riddle had raised this issue of exclusion at almost every convention of the ANA but to no avail. The integration of African-American nurses into the Army and Navy Nurse Corps, however, had had an effect on the way African-American nurses were perceived and the ANA was finally forced to redefine its position.

In 1948, the ANA announced that it would open membership to African-American nurses. The news was stunning. One African-American nurse commented, "Those of us who know the ugly sting of prejudice will gather courage from this hopeful step by the ANA." [185] Since the days when Mary Eliza Mahoney had earned her degree, African-American nurses had waited for this final mark of integration—membership in the most important association of their profession.

For Mabel Staupers, this news meant that the work and mission of the NACGN had been accomplished. Most state nursing associations now admitted African-American nurses, and a majority of nursing schools now admitted students regardless of race. In January of 1951, the NACGN issues a press release announcing that the National Association of Colored Graduate Nurses had been dissolved by a vote of its board of directors and members. "The doors have been opened and the black nurse has been given a seat in the top councils," said Staupers. She added, "We are now part of the great organization of nurses, the American Nurses' Association." [186]

Current Challenges

8

MODERN PIONEERS

In her essay entitled "The History of African-Americans in White," Ann Waterman explained that most African-American pioneers of nursing are still largely unknown and their achievements unrecognized:

> Even the general populace knows the name of the famous British nurse, Florence Nightingale[,] but do they recognize the names of Mary Eliza Mahoney or Adah Belle Samuel Thoms? These two women were also famous and pioneered nursing in the late 1800's and early 1900's. I would propose that even most nurses in this country have no idea what these two women accomplished in their lifetime.[187]

Among heroines and pioneers in the nursing profession are some whose names may not be as famous as Mahoney's and Thoms's. One of these was Gladys Callendar, who, when she passed away in 1998 at the age of 95, was the oldest member of the Black Nurses Association. Callendar earned her nursing degree from the University of Michigan and became a registered nurse in the mid-1920s; she later became the first African-American nursing supervisor at the Health Department in Cincinnati, Ohio, where she worked for over 40 years. The local community recognized her efforts with a series of awards, including a Trailblazer Award from the West End Health Center in 1996; the *Cincinnati Enquirer* named her "Woman of the Year" in 1971.[188]

In Baltimore, Maryland, Mimi Bailey carved out a reputation herself and became a local legend. In 1958, she was the first African-American nurse hired by Montebello State Hospital where she worked for several years. Her history is amazing. She once worked as a railroad laborer and, since her retirement from nursing, she has worked as a volunteer, logging more than 30,000 hours at a local senior citizens' center.[189]

Another modern heroine is M. Elizabeth Carnegie. Carnegie earned her nursing degree in 1937 from the Lincoln School for Nurses in New York City, the same school that showed so much support to the NACGN. She continued her education, earning a bachelor's degree in sociology and a master's degree, as well as a doctoral degree, in public administration. Since the 1970s, she has been a renowned scholar and historian of African-American nursing; she has served as editor of *Nursing Research* and has written several books, including *The Path We Tread: Blacks in Nursing, 1854–1990*. She has been awarded six honorary doctorates, and she was inducted into the American Nurses Association Hall of Fame in 2001.[190] Each year, Howard University holds an M. Elizabeth Carnegie Annual Nursing Research Conference to support scholarship in the field of nursing.[191]

PROBLEMS CONTINUE

Conditions have certainly improved in recent years for African-American nurses. Some news, however, seems to arrive well beyond the time it was expected. Mabel Staupers, the dynamic executive director of the NACGN, was inducted into the Nurses Hall of Fame in 1996. The Hall of Fame is organized by the American Nurses Association, which once shunned African-American nurses who sought admission. At the posthumous induction ceremony, an ANA spokesperson described Staupers as "a leader of vision determination and courage [who] helped break down color barriers in nursing at a time when segregation was entrenched in this country."[192]

Unfortunately, problems for African-American nurses continue to exist today. Damon Adams, writing in the *American Medical News*, has noted:

> A new survey about minority nurses shows that many of these nurses believe there are personal and professional barriers to their progress and that they have been denied

promotions because of race. African-American nurses were more likely than other respondents to say they were denied promotions for jobs for which they were qualified. Such problems make it harder to attract minorities to nursing, according to some minority nursing leaders.[193]

The results of the survey, which was conducted by the American Nurses Federation in 2000, surprised many: "A majority of African-Americans, Hispanics and Asian-

A Continuing Battle

The history of African-American women in nursing demonstrates that the road was paved by inspiring and pioneering women, such as Mahoney. Today, the battle for inclusion in the nursing field is far from over.

The number of African-American women in nursing continues to steadily increase—it rose 119 percent between the years 1980 and 2000.* Furthermore, African-American women continue to break barriers in the nursing profession. For example, in 1999, Elnora Daniel was elected President of Chicago State University—the first African-American nurse to become the president of a major American university.** (For more information on Elnora Daniel, enter her name into any search engine and browse the sites listed.)

Despite these signs of progress, the overall rate of African Americans in nursing remains quite low. Of the nation's 1.3 million nurses, only 5 percent are African American.***

The only reasons that can be ascertained for such low numbers are ongoing discrimination and racism in the field. The problem is not just an American issue; in England, studies report that black nurses are twice as likely as white nurses to be underpaid and far less likely to be promoted to higher positions.+

Americans/Pacific Islanders attributed denial of promotion to their race rather than to experience or education."[194] Clearly, although African-American nurses have been integrated into the profession, many obstacles still remain in their path.

MARY ELIZA MAHONEY AWARD

Mary Eliza Mahoney is still recognized as the one who started it all—the first African-American woman to break down the barrier and gain admittance to the nursing profession. The

Other reasons for low numbers of African-American women in nursing are detailed by Hilda Richards, President of the National Black Nurses Association (NBNA), who explains that African-American women need "emotional and financial support" while they are on the road to obtaining their degrees. Furthermore, African-American women who are single parents need help with childcare. Finally, the pressures of living in urban America are a daily challenge faced by African-American women. All of these factors combine to inhibit African-American women from realizing their potential in the nursing field.++

* Janet Wells, "Great Leaps, Step by Step." Nurseweek.com. December 16, 2003. *http://www.nurseweek.com/news/features/03-12/africanamerRN_print.html* (Retrieved February 18, 2004).

** Ibid.

*** Ibid.

+ Jo Revill, "Black nurses paid less than white colleagues ." The Observer. February 8, 2004. *http://observer.guardian.co.uk/uk_news/story/0,6903,1143512,00.html* (Retrieved February 21, 2004).

++ Sylvia Coleman, "Black History Month Special: Remembering Trailblazers & a Look at Black Nurses Today." Advance for Nurses. *http://www.advancefornurses.com/common/editorial/editorial.aspx?CC=9588* (Retrieved February 20, 2004).

National Association of Colored Graduate Nurses recognized this fact by establishing, in 1936, the Mary Mahoney Award, an annual prize awarded to African-American nurses who have demonstrated excellence in their field. The first award recipient was Adah Belle Samuels Thoms, who was honored in 1936. Helen Miller, who dedicated much time to researching the life of Mahoney, received the award in 1968. When the NACGN merged with the American Nurses Association, the ANA agreed to continue to distribute the award each year, which it does to this day.

In recent years, thanks to the help of nursing historians and an interest in the history of African-American women in nursing, Mary Eliza Mahoney's contribution has received new appreciation. She was named to the Nursing Hall of Fame in 1976 and to the National Women's Hall of Fame in 1993.[195]

Mahoney's impact on the field of nursing for African-American women was manifold. Althea T. Davis aptly wrote: "Mahoney was a role model for the black nurse and for nurses of all races. In addition to her obvious role as an architect of integration and equality, Mahoney was an inspiration and a symbol for black nurses and the NACGN. . . . She was revered and respected."[196]

1820   Florence Nightingale, the first professional nurse, is born in England

1845   Mary Eliza Mahoney, the first professional African-American nurse, is born in Massachusetts

1854   Florence Nightingale proves the effectiveness of professional nursing by dramatically lowering the casualty rate of British soldiers during the Crimean War

Timeline

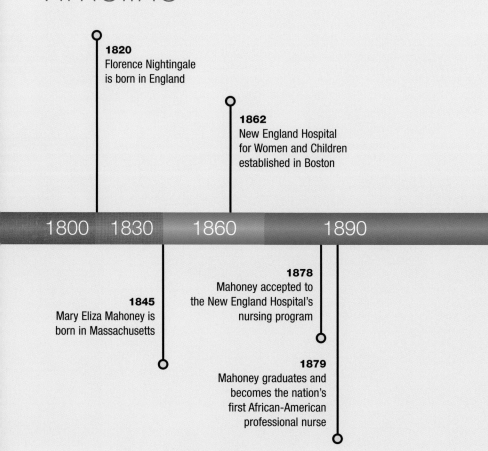

1820
Florence Nightingale
is born in England

1862
New England Hospital
for Women and Children
established in Boston

1800   1830   1860   1890

1878
Mahoney accepted to
the New England Hospital's
nursing program

1845
Mary Eliza Mahoney is
born in Massachusetts

1879
Mahoney graduates and
becomes the nation's
first African-American
professional nurse

1860 The Nightingale nursing schools are established, training nurses in professional medical care of patients

1861 Civil War erupts between northern and southern states. African-American women, including Sojourner Truth and Harriet Tubman, serve as nurses, despite a lack of professional training

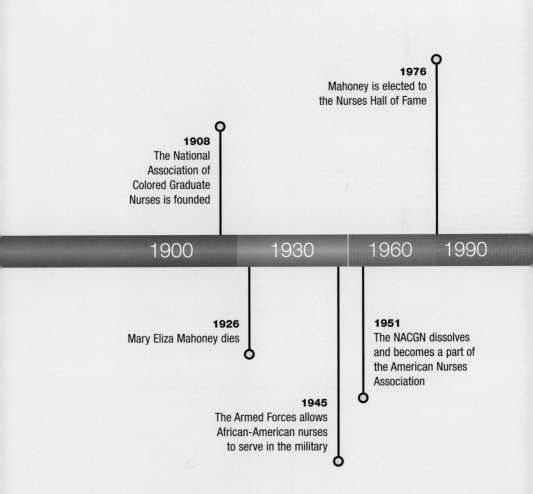

1976
Mahoney is elected to the Nurses Hall of Fame

1908
The National Association of Colored Graduate Nurses is founded

1900   1930   1960   1990

1926
Mary Eliza Mahoney dies

1951
The NACGN dissolves and becomes a part of the American Nurses Association

1945
The Armed Forces allows African-American nurses to serve in the military

Chronology

1862 New England Hospital for Women and Children founded in Boston by Dr. Zakrzewska; the Civil War makes the need for professional nurses evident, and the New England Hospital institutes a nursing program

1878 Mahoney accepted to the nursing program at the New England Hospital for Women and Children—the first African-American woman to enroll

1879 Mahoney graduates from the program and becomes the nation's first African-American professional nurse. She enters a private nursing practice

1908 The National Association of Colored Graduate Nurses is founded by Martha Minerva Franklin and other African American nursing professionals. Mary Eliza Mahoney participates in establishing the NACGN in its early years

1914 During World War I, the United States Armed Forces bars African American nurses from serving in the military and treating white American soldiers

1916 Adah Belle Samuels Thoms is elected president of the NACGN and revives the organization's goal of becoming assimilated into the nursing field

1926 Mahoney dies of complications from breast cancer

1931 Estelle Massey Riddle Osborne becomes the first African American woman to earn a Master's degree in nursing. She recruits Mabel Staupers, and the two become a changing force in the NACGN

1934 Estelle Massey Riddle Osborne elected president of the NACGN

1936 The NACGN announces its annual Mary Eliza Mahoney Award, given to an African American nurse who demonstrates high standards and excellence in the profession

1945 The Armed Forces ends it quota system and allows African-American nurses to serve in the military during World War II

1951	Since African American nurses are now accepted in the military and for membership in the ANA, the NACGN dissolves and becomes a part of the American Nurses Association
1973	Mary Eliza Mahoney is memorialized with a ceremony and a commemorative statue on her gravesite in Boston's suburbs
1976	Interest in Mahoney's life and contributions to nursing is renewed, and Mahoney is elected to the Nurses Hall of Fame
1993	Mahoney is elected to the National Women's Hall of Fame

Notes

Chapter 1

1. *The New American Desk Encyclopedia.* Meridian Books, 3rd edition. March 1994. p. 1122.

2. Cathy N. Davidson, and Linda Wagner-Martin, Eds. *The Oxford Companion to Women's Writing in the United States* (New York: Oxford University Press, 1995), p. 4.

3. *The New American Desk Encyclopedia.* Meridian Books, 3rd edition. March 1994. p. 10.

4. Frederick Douglass, *The Narrative of the Life of Frederick Douglass, an American Slave.* In *The Classic Slave Narratives.* Edited by Henry Louis Gates, Jr. (New York: Penguin Books, 1987), p. 274.

5. Ibid., p. 275.

6. *Microsoft® Encarta® Online Encyclopedia 2003,* http://encarta.msn.com, "Civil War, American."

7. Davidson, p. 4.

8. Ibid., p. 4.

9. Ibid., p. 4.

10. Ibid., pp. 856–857.

11. M.E. Doona, "Glimpses of Mary Eliza Mahoney" (7 May 1845–4 January 1929). *Journal of Nursing History.* 1(2):20–34, 1986, p. 22.

12. "Boston-Historical Context." http://www.soulofamerica.com/cityfldr/boston1.html.

13. Miller, Helen S. *Mary Eliza Mahoney, 1845–1926: America's First Black Professional Nurse, A Historical Perspective.* Atlanta, GA: Wright Pub. Co., 1986, p. 3.

14. Ibid., p. 12.

15. Ibid., p. 4.

16. Ibid., p. 4.

17. Ibid., p. 5.

18. Doona, p. 22.

19. Miller, p. 9.

20. Ibid., p. 10.

21. Ibid., p. 12.

22. Doona, pp. 21, 22.

23. Miller, pp. 12–13.

24. Ibid., p. 13.

25. *Microsoft® Encarta® Online Encyclopedia 2003,* http://encarta.msn.com, "Civil War, American."

26. Ibid.

27. Ibid.

Chapter 2

28. Darlene Stille, *Extraordinary Women of Medicine* (New York: Children's Press, 1997), p. 29.

29. Patricia Donahue, *Nursing, The Finest Art: An Illustrated History* (St. Louis, MO: Mosby, 1996), p. 199.

30. Stille, p. 30.

31. Ibid., p. 31.

32. Donahue, p. 200.

33. Stille, p. 31.

34. Donahue, p. 201.

35. Ibid., p. 201.

36. Ibid., p. 201.

37. Ibid., p. 204.

38. Quoted in Donahue, p. 204.

39. Ibid., pp. 207–208.

40. Quoted in Stille, p. 35.

41. Stille p. 77.

42. Ibid., p. 78.

43. Ibid., p. 79.

44. Donahue, p. 270.

45. Miller, p. 20.

46. Donahue, p. 270.

47. Ibid., p. 270.

48. Ibid., p. 270.

49. Stille, p. 79.

50. Miller, p. 19.

51. Ibid., p. 20.

52. Ibid., p. 19.

53. Doona, p. 23.

54. Ibid., p. 23.

Chapter 3

55. Donahue, p. 246.

56. Ibid., p. 247.

57. Ibid., p. 258.

58. Ibid., p. 258.

59. Quoted in Donahue, p. 259.

60. Donahue, p. 252.

61. Jenn Bumb, "Dorothea Dix reformed treatment of the mentally ill." *Human Quest* (St. Petersburg: Sep/Oct 2003), Vol. 217, Iss. 5, p. 19. (Retrieved December 10, 2003 from ProQuest Database).

62. Althea T. Davis, Early Black American Leaders in Nursing: Architects for Integration and Equality (Boston: Jones and Bartlett Publishers, 1999), p. 18.

63. Quoted in Sojourner Truth, "Ain't I a Woman?" Adapted to poetry by Erlene Stetson. In *Ain't I a Woman!: A Book of Women's Poetry from Around the World.* Edited by Illona Linthwaite (New York: Wings Books, 1990), pp. 129–130.

64. "Emancipation at Arlington: Freedman's Village, 1863," *http://www.nps.gov/arho/tour/ history/arlingtoninbetween3.html.*

65. Davis, p. 180.

66. Ibid., p. 18.

67. Davidson, pp. 888–889.

68. Davis, p. 19.

69. Ibid., p. 17.

70. Ibid., p. 17.

71. Miller, p. 10.

72. Ibid., p. 10.

73. Doona, p. 24.

74. Ibid., pp. 23–24.

75. Donahue, p. 271.

76. Miller, p. 12.

77. Stille, p. 24.

78. Doona, p. 24.

Chapter 4

79. Miller, p. 20.

80. Ibid., p. 21.

81. Ibid., p. 21.

82. Quoted in Donahue, p. 270.

83. Miller, p. 20.

84. Doona, p. 26.

85. Ibid., p. 24.

86. Stille, p. 111.

87. Doona, p. 26.

88. Miller, p. 21.

89. Doona, p. 26.

90. Ibid., p. 27.

91. Miller, p. 21.

92. Ibid., p. 21.

Notes

93. Ibid., p. 21.

94. Davis, p. 50.

95. Miller, p. 30.

96. Ibid., p. 29.

97. Ibid., p. 30.

98. Ibid., p. 26.

99. Ibid., p. 30.

100. Ibid., pp. 101–102.

101. Ibid., p. 103.

102. Miller, pp. 102–103.

103. Ibid., p. 108.

104. Ibid., p. 172.

Chapter 5

105. "Etched in Stone"
*http://www.nursing.upenn.edu/
history/Chronicle/F98/franklin.htm*
(Retrieved December 12, 2003).

106. Donahue, p. 271.

107. Hodge, Jacqueline. "Black
Women's Military Contributions."
Retrieved on May 25, 2004.
*http://userpages.aug.com/captbarb/
contributions.html.*

108. Sheldon, Kathryn. "Brief History
of Black Women in the Military."
Women in Military Service for
America Memorial Foundation
Homepage. Retrieved on May 25,
2004. *http://www.womensmemo-
rial.org/Education/BBH1998.html.*

109. Hodge, Jacqueline. "Black
Women's Military Contributions."
Retrieved on May 25, 2004.
*http://userpages.aug.com/captbarb/
contributions.html.*

110. Davis, p. 76.

111. Ibid., p. 76.

112. Ibid., p. 101.

113. Ibid., p. 105.

114. Quoted in Davis, p. 105.

115. Davis, p. 105.

116. "History of Lincoln Medical and
Mental Health Center," *http://
linmed.org/history_of_lincoln_med
ical_and_m.htm* (Retrieved
December 10, 2003).

117. Davis, p. 106.

118. Quoted in Davis, p. 107.

119. Davis, p. 107.

120. Ibid., p. 107.

121. Ibid., p. 107.

122. Ibid., p. 108.

123. Quoted in Davis, p. 108.

124. Ibid., p. 77.

125. Ibid., p. 77.

126. New York Public Library. National
Association of Colored Graduate
Nurses Records, 1908–1951.
Manuscripts, Archives and Rare
Books Division.

127. Davis, p. 110.

128. African American Registry,
"National Association of Colored
Graduate Nurses Founded!"
www.africanamericanregistry.com.

129. Ibid.

130. Quoted in Davis, 82.

131. Davis, 112.

132. Darlene Clark Hine, *Black Women
in White: Racial Conflict and
Cooperation in the Nursing Profession, 1890–1950* (Bloomington,
IN: Indiana University Press,
1989), p. 100.

133. Ibid., p. 93.

134. Ibid., p. 93.

135. Ibid., p. 99.

136. Ibid., p. 99.

137. Quoted in Hine, p. 100.

138. Hine, p. 109.

139. Ibid., p. 108.

140. Ibid., p. 100.

141. Davis, p. 150.

142. Ibid., p. 149.

143. Davis, p. 112.

Chapter 6

144. Quoted in Davis, p. 113.

145. Quoted in Davis, p. 115.

146. *Microsoft® Encarta® Online Encyclopedia 2004*, s.v. "World War I" (by William Keylor) *http://encarta.msn.com.*

147. Quoted in Hine, p. 103.

148. Davis, p. 115.

149. Ibid., p. 119.

150. Hine, pp. 103–104.

151. Quoted in Davis, p. 120.

152. Hine, p. 100.

153. Ibid., p. 100.

154. Ibid., p. 118.

155. Ibid., p. 118.

156. Ibid., p. 119.

157. Ibid., p. 64.

158. Ibid., pp. 119–120.

159. Ibid., p. 120.

160. Ibid., p. 120.

161. "Mabel Staupers," Gale Group Bio.

162. Sylvia Coleman, "Black History Month Special: Remembering Trailblazers & a Look at Black Nurses Today." *http://www.advancefornurses.com/common/editorial/editorial.aspx?CC=9588* (Retrieved February 20, 2004).

163. Hine, p. 110.

164. Davis, p. 150.

165. "National Association of Colored Graduate Nurses founded!" African American Registry. *http://www.aaregistry.com.*

166. Davis, p. 88.

167. Hine, p. 111.

168. Ibid., p. 111.

169. Ibid., p. 116.

170. Ibid., p. 116.

171. Ibid., pp. 116–117.

Chapter 7

172. Hine, p. 162.

173. Quoted in Hine, p. 164.

174. Hine, p. 166.

175. Quoted in Hine, p. 166.

176. Quoted in Hine, p. 167.

177. Quoted in Hine, p. 166.

178. Quoted in Hine, p. 168.

179. Hine, p. 170.

180. Hine, pp. 170–173.

181. Quoted in Hine, p. 178.

182. Quoted in Hine, p. 179.

183. Hine, p. 179.

184. Quoted in Hine, p. 180.

185. Quoted in Hine, p. 183.

186. Quoted in Hine, p. 185.

Notes

Chapter 8

187. Ann Waterman, "The History of African-Americans in White," *http://www.coe.ohio-state.edu/edpl/gordon/courses/863/nurses.html* (Retrieved January 2, 2004).

188. "Gladys Callendar, blazed trail for African-American nurses." Cincinnati Post (Cincinnati, Ohio: *Sep 26, 1998*), p. 12.A.

189. Shapiro, "Don't look for Mimi Bailey in a miniskirt." *The Sun* (Baltimore, Md.: Jan 23, 1997), p. 4.E.

190. Buczek, SUNY Honors Two Women Black History Month Event Features an Alabama Medical Director and an Author. Black History Month Series. *The Post-Standard.* (Syracuse, N.Y.: Feb 22, 2001), p. B.3.

191. Powell et al, "Socializing students: Toward a career in nursing research." *Nursing Education Perspectives* (New York: Mar/Apr 2002), Vol. 23, Iss. 2; p. 76.

192. Bourne, "Mabel Staupers installed in nurses' hall of fame." *New York Amsterdam News.* (New York, N.Y.: Jun 22, 1996), pp. 9, 10.

193. Damon Adams, "Survey says minority nursing bias hampers advancement." *American Medical News* (Chicago: Mar 11, 2002), Vol. 45, Iss. 10; pg. 22, 1 p. Retrieved January 10, 2003 from ProQuest Database.

194. Adams, p. 22.

195. *http://wwwa.search.eb.com/women/articles/Mahoney_Mary.html.*

196. Davis, p. 144.

Adams, Damon. "Survey says minority nursing bias hampers advancement." *American Medical News.* Chicago: Mar 11, 2002. Vol. 45, Iss. 10; p. 22, 1 pg. Retrieved January 10, 2003 from ProQuest Database.

"Anna Eleanor Roosevelt." White House web site. *http://www.whitehouse.gov/history/firstladies/ar32.html.*

Bourne, St. Clair T. "Mabel Staupers installed in nurses' hall of fame." *New York Amsterdam News.* New York, N.Y.: Jun 22, 1996. pg. 9, 10. Retrieved from December 10, 2003 from ProQuest Database.

Buczek, Nancy. SUNY Honors Two Women Black History Month Event Features an Alabama Medical Director and an Author. Black History Month Series. *The Post-Standard.* Syracuse, N.Y.: Feb 22, 2001. p. B.3. Retrieved December 10, 2003, from ProQuest Database.

Bumb, Jenn. "Dorothea Dix reformed treatment of the mentally ill." Human Quest. St. Petersburg: Sep/Oct 2003. Vol. 217, Iss. 5; p. 19. Retrieved December 10, 2003 from ProQuest Database.

Burgess, May Ayres, ed. *Nurses, Patients, and Pocketbooks: A Study of the Economics of Nursing.* The Committee on the Grading of Nursing Schools. 1928. Reprinted by Garland Books: New York, 1984.

Carruthers, Evelyn. "Nursing," Microsoft® Encarta® Online Encyclopedia 2004 *http://encarta.msn.com* © 1997–2004 Microsoft Corporation.

"Civil War, American." Microsoft® Encarta® Online Encyclopedia 2003.

"Civil War Nurses." *http://www.civilwarhome.com/civilwarnurses.htm* (Retrieved December 4, 2003).

Coleman, Sylvia. "Black History Month Special: Remembering Trailblazers & a Look at Black Nurses Today." *http://www.advancefornurses.com/common/editorial/editorial.aspx?CC=9588* (Retrieved February 20, 2004).

Cox, Clinton. *African American Healers.* Black Stars Series. Jim Haskins, General Editor. New York: John Wiley and Sons, 2000.

Davidson, Cathy N, and Linda Wagner-Martin, Eds. *The Oxford Companion to Women's Writing in the United States.* New York: Oxford University Press, 1995.

Davis, Althea T. *Early Black American Leaders in Nursing: Architects for Integration and Equality.* Boston: Jones and Bartlett Publishers, 1999.

Donahue, Patricia. *Nursing, The Finest Art: An Illustrated History.* Mosby Pub, 1996.

Bibliography

Doona, M.E. "Glimpses of Mary Eliza Mahoney (7 May 1845–4 January 1929)." *Journal of Nursing History.* 1(2):20–34, 1986.

Douglass, Frederick. *The Narrative of the Life of Frederick Douglass, an American Slave.* In *The Classic Slave Narratives.* Edited by Henry Louis Gates, Jr. New York: Penguin Books, 1987.

"Emancipation at Arlington: Freedmen's Village, 1863." *http://www.nps.gov/arho/tour/history/arlingtoninbetween3.html.* (Retrieved January 2, 2003).

"Etched in Stone." Retrieved December 12, 2003 from *http://www.nursing.upenn.edu/history/Chronicle/F98/franklin.htm.*

"Gladys Callendar, blazed trail for African-American nurses." Cincinnati Post. Cincinnati, Ohio: Sep 26, 1998. pg. 12.A. (Retrieved January 4, 2003, from ProQuest Database).

"Harlem History." *http://www.harlemspirituals.com/harlem.html* (Retrieved February 20, 2004).

"History of Lincoln Medical and Mental Health Center." *http://linmed.org/history_of_lincoln_medical_and_m.htm* (Retrieved December 10, 2003).

Keylor, William. "World War I." Microsoft® Encarta® Online Encyclopedia 2004 *http://encarta.msn.com.*

"Life of Harriet Tubman, The." New York History Net. *http://www.nyhistory.com/harriettubman/life.htm* (Retrieved February 19, 2004).

"National Association of Colored Graduate Nurses founded!" African American Registry. *www.aaregistry.com.*

New York Public Library. National Association of Colored Graduate Nurses Records, 1908–1951. Manuscripts, Archives and Rare Books Division.

Powell, Dorothy L., Pauline M. Green, and Diann S. Slade. "Socializing students: Toward a career in nursing research." *Nursing Education Perspectives.* New York: Mar/Apr 2002. Vol. 23, Iss. 2; pg. 76, 5 pgs. (Retrieved December 10, 2003 from ProQuest Database).

Revill, Jo. "Black nurses paid less than white colleagues." *The Observer.* February 8, 2004. *http://observer.guardian.co.uk/uk_news/story/0,6903,1143512,00.html.* (Retrieved February 21, 2004).

Shapiro, Stephanie. "Don't look for Mimi Bailey in a miniskirt." *The Sun.* Baltimore, Md.: Jan 23, 1997. p. 4.E. Retrieved January 10, 2003, from ProQuest Database.

"Souls of America." *http://www.soul ofamerica.com/cityfldr/boston1.html* (Retrieved on October 26, 2003).

"Staupers, Mabel." *http://search.eb.com /blackhistory/micro/727/72.html* (Retrieved January 2, 2003).

Stille, Darlene. *Extraordinary Women of Medicine.* New York: Children's Press, 1997.

Truth, Sojourner. "Ain't I a Woman?" Adapted to poetry by Erlene Stetson. In *Ain't I a Woman!: A Book of Women's Poetry From Around the World.* Edited by Illona Linthwaite. New York: Wings Books, 1990.

"Voices from the Past, Visions of the Future." American Nurses Association web site. *http://nursingworld.org/centenn/index.htm* (Retrieved February 18, 2004).

Waterman, Ann. "The History of African-Americans in White." *http://www. coe.ohio-state.edu/edpl/gordon/courses/863/nurses.html* (Retrieved January 2, 2004).

Wells, Janet. "Great Leaps, Step by Step." Nurseweek.com. December 16, 2003. *http://www.nurseweek.com/news/features/03-12/africanamerRN_ print.html* (Retrieved February 18, 2004).

Further Reading

"Black Nurses in History: A Bibliography and Guide to Web Resources." University of Medicine and Dentistry of New Jersey. *http://www4.umdnj. edu/camlbweb/blacknurses.html.*

Cox, Clinton. *African American Healers.* Black Stars Series. Jim Haskins, General Editor. New York: John Wiley and Sons, 2000.

Davis, Althea T. *Early Black American Leaders in Nursing: Architects for Integration and Equality.* Boston: Jones and Bartlett Publishers, 1999.

Hine, Darlene Clark. *Black Women in White: Racial Conflict and Cooperation in the Nursing Profession, 1890–1950.* Bloomington, IN: Indiana University Press, 1989.

"Mahoney, Mary." Women in American History. Encyclopedia Britannica website. *http://wwwa.search.eb.com/women/articles/MahoneyMary.html* (Retrieved February 18, 2004).

"Mary Eliza Mahoney." American Nurses Association Hall of Fame. *http://www.nursingworld.org/hof/mahome.htm.*

"Mary Eliza Mahoney." Bridgewater State College Hall of Black Achievement. *http://www.bridgew.edu/HOBA/Inductees/Mahoney.htm.*

Miller, Helen S. *Mary Eliza Mahoney, 1845–1926: America's First Black Professional Nurse, A Historical Perspective.* 1984.

Index

About the Author

Susan Muaddi Darraj (http://www.SusanMuaddiDarraj.com) is a freelance writer based in Baltimore, Maryland. She edits *The Baltimore Review*, a national literary journal, and teaches English and writing at Hartford Community College.